Forts of Florida

UNIVERSITY PRESS OF FLORIDA

Florida A&M University, Tallahassee
Florida Atlantic University, Boca Raton
Florida Gulf Coast University, Ft. Myers
Florida International University, Miami
Florida State University, Tallahassee
New College of Florida, Sarasota
University of Central Florida, Orlando
University of Florida, Gainesville
University of North Florida, Jacksonville
University of South Florida, Tampa
University of West Florida, Pensacola

Rodney Carlisle and Loretta Carlisle

University Press of Florida
Gainesville · Tallahassee · Tampa · Boca Raton
Pensacola · Orlando · Miami · Jacksonville · Ft. Myers · Sarasota

Forts of Florida

A Guidebook

Printed in the United States of America on acid-free paper.

17 16 15 14 13 12 6 5 4 3 2 1

A copy of cataloging-in-publication data is available from
the Library of Congress.
ISBN 978-0-8130-4012-7

University Press of Florida
15 Northwest 15th Street
Gainesville, FL 32611-2079
http://www.upf.com

For Taylor McEvoy, our granddaughter

Contents

Part 3. Central Florida

Part 4. South Florida

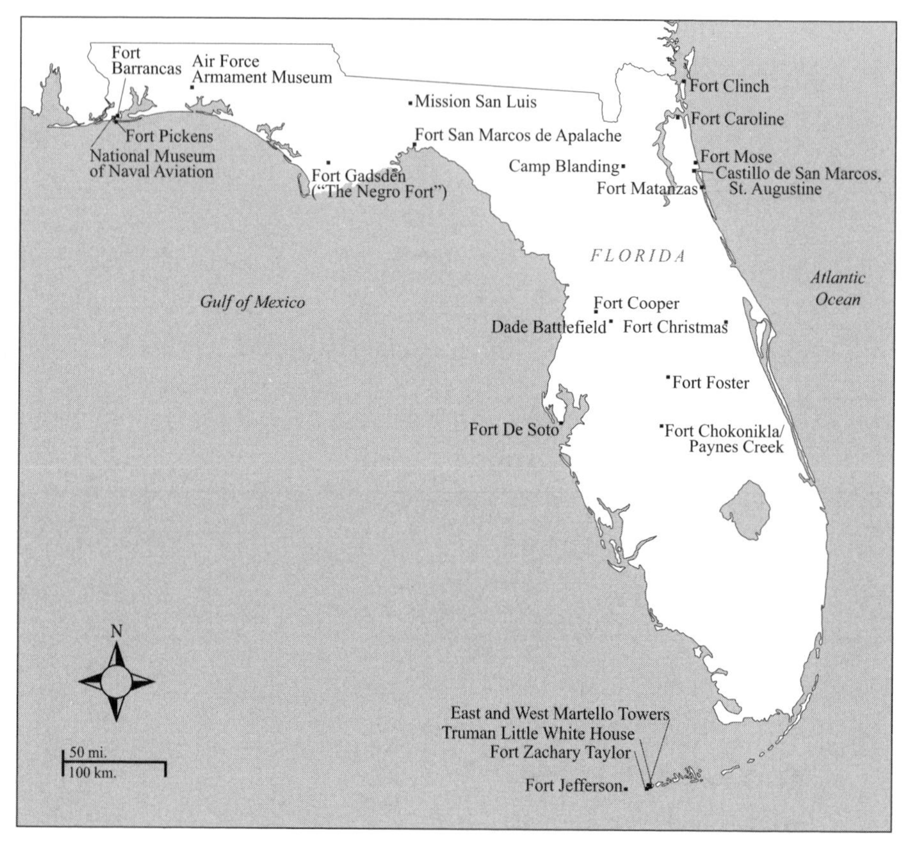

Locations of the twenty-three featured military sites and forts that can be enjoyed by visitors. Though the state once was home to scores of occupied forts, most of them have vanished over the course of Florida's long history. (Map by Tracy Smith.)

Introduction

This guidebook tells the stories of twenty-three military sites in Florida. These forts and military museums are all places that can be visited, and many of them are among the state's most popular tourist destinations. Although in the long history of Florida, at least another one hundred other forts were at one time or another built and occupied in the state, each of these historic and present-day forts has a story to tell to the visitor. The other forts, most now long-vanished, are sometimes marked only by a single sign, or commemorated only in a place-name (such as Fort Myers or Fort Lauderdale). Some listings by historians show another two hundred or so temporary encampments, many of which have not been located. Although all of those places played a part in the history of Florida, this guidebook focuses on places where original structures, reconstructions, ruins, museums, or visitor centers are there to tell the story.

The unique story of Florida's military history is revealed in the fort structures and in the museums maintained at the sites presented here. Although the locations of some of the vanished forts are marked with plaques or historical markers, the forts listed in this guidebook have informative displays and actual or replica structures to explore.

As a guidebook, this volume is written with the visitor in mind, providing practical information such as the days and hours of operation, contact information, fees charged, and notable annual special events. The entries include unique facts and information about what is available at the site and direct readers to nearby points of interest. Each of the forts, parks, or battlefields has a rich history, compiled here from the research of numerous local, state, and military historians and presented in a condensed few paragraphs within each entry. At the end of the volume, we include a glossary that defines many of the military and historical presentation terms visitors might encounter as they visit the sites, a chronology of events related to the forts' histories, as well as a list of further readings for those who want to learn more about Florida military history or about fort construction.

We have toured each of the sites described here, and the modern photographs you see in this work were all taken by Loretta Carlisle. The maps and line drawings have been gleaned from documentary sources. The writing results from a year of research studying documents, old maps, historical monographs, and the rich sources of information available on the Internet.

The military history of Florida produces a series of surprises for those who have learned U.S. history from textbooks and survey classes in high school or college. Unlike the original thirteen colonies, Florida was not a British colony except for a short period of twenty years, 1763–83. Although the Spanish recaptured West Florida from the British in 1781, the main peninsula of Florida, known as British East Florida, remained under British control until the articles of peace between Spain and Britain in 1783. Aside from this relatively brief eighteen to twenty years under the British, the Spanish had ruled Florida since the sixteenth century (first settled long before Plymouth Colony in Massachusetts or Jamestown in Virginia), defending the settlement in numerous little-remembered battles with French and British colonial forces.

The French-built Fort Caroline, near Jacksonville, the massive Spanish Castillo de San Marcos at St. Augustine, Mission San Luis in Tallahassee, Fort Matanzas at the southern tip of Anastasia Island, and the first free African American community at Fort Mose, just north of St. Augustine, all tell aspects of that early story. The tales include massacres, battles, sieges, pirates, Indians, fugitive slaves, and desperate overland marches in blazing heat. At these forts, you will uncover information about the

The first European impressions of the Timucua Indians in Florida were recorded in engravings such as this one showing methods of killing alligators. (1591 engraving by Theodor de Bry, after a watercolor by Jacques Le Moyne. Courtesy of the Library of Congress.)

earliest Timucua and Apalachee Indians who lived in Florida before the arrival of Europeans and Seminoles, the story of the War of Jenkins' Ear, and learn of the unique natural building material known as coquina, mined from compacted shell deposits near the coast. St. Augustine itself, the oldest European-built town in the continental United States, is at the center of many these early stories.

Florida's history reflects as much conflict as that of any part of the United States. Although today, pirate stories are little more than fanciful tales and pirate relics are almost all commercialized, tongue-in-cheek kitsch, early Florida did, in fact, provide refuge for several notorious real pirates. Pirates and adventurers established small independent states for various periods of time, at remote locations such as that of Gregor MacGregor, and later Luis Aury on Amelia Island in northeast Florida in 1817, or the "Muskogee Nation" under the leadership of British Loyalist William Bowles near Tallahassee in 1795–1800.

As slavery expanded in South Carolina, Georgia, and then to the "Old Southwest" of Alabama and Mississippi, Florida represented an escape route for fugitive slaves, an underground railroad that ran *south*, not north, to freedom. The Spanish welcomed freedom-seeking African Americans, and later the Seminole Indians of Florida gave haven to escaped slaves. The Seminoles themselves had fled as refugees and settlers from Upper Creek and Lower Creek (Mikasuki- and Hitchiti-speaking Muscogee) tribes to the north. Perhaps because African Americans and Native Americans ran that southern freedom trail rather than northern abolitionist whites, the story of that route to freedom did not quite fit into the traditional mythology of American history. Slaves had been escaping into Florida as early as the 1680s, even before the Seminoles moved to the area; up to 1763, they fled primarily to St. Augustine and joined the growing community of free people of color under Spanish authority who became the settlers at Fort Mose. After 1800, slaves continued to flee into Florida, and at that time they often went into the towns and territory of the Seminoles. Escaping African Americans not only took refuge in Florida, but they armed themselves to protect against slave catchers. This story of African Americans' armed resistance to slavery and to the forces that supported slavery has been relegated to footnotes in most U.S. history textbooks, but has in recent years been the subject of many exciting historical studies.

During Queen Anne's War (1702–13), which involved British-French conflicts along the border between what is now the United States and Canada, British forces invaded Spanish Florida, destroying long-established Spanish missions among the Native American Apalachee people in the northwest part of the territory. The Apalachee, who had lived peaceably under Spanish civil and religious authority in the region, fled, burning their mission, community, and fortress at San Luis.

More than a century later, in northwest Florida, at a site southwest of Tallahassee known as the "Negro Fort," and later as Fort Gadsden, the black freedom fighters occupied a British fort that was targeted in a raid led by Duncan L. Clinch in 1816, a raid

Lithograph of a Seminole village as depicted in the mid-1830s. (T. F. Gray and James, Charleston, S.C., 1837. Courtesy of the Library of Congress.)

later disavowed by the U.S. government. Tragically, a hot shot from a U.S. barge in the Apalachicola River exploded the fort's powder magazine, killing 270 of 300 men, women, and children inside the fort. Andrew Jackson's invasion of Florida, and his capture and execution of two British citizens two years later at Fort San Marcos de Apalache, helped precipitate the Spanish decision to transfer title of all of Florida to the United States in 1821. While the remnants of these forts are now just partially overgrown foundation ruins, they mark crucial points in this little-remembered history of U.S. expansion into Florida.

As settlers from Georgia, Alabama, and other states to the north moved into Florida in the following decades to expand cattle ranches, sugar plantations, and to take the best land for other crops, they encountered dozens of small settlements of the Seminoles, who had quickly learned farming, cattle raising, wooden-frame house construction, and the value of firearms for defense. And living with the Seminoles were thousands of African Americans, refugees from the states to the north, with their children. Some of these people were of pure African ancestry; others were the offspring of Seminole-African marriages.

"Osceola of Florida / drawn on stone by George Catlin, from his original portrait," 1838. (Courtesy of the Library of Congress.)

As white settlers pushed in, they refused to recognize the right of Seminoles and their African American allies to live and farm the land. Most whites believed that Native Americans were all savages, and regarded the African Americans among them as runaways who could be captured and returned to their former owners for a cash reward or sold at a healthy profit.

By the 1830s, after Andrew Jackson became president, he enforced the U.S. Indian removal policy that led to the notorious Trail of Tears, in which thousands of Native Americans from Georgia, Alabama, and Mississippi were marched westward to reservations in Indian Territory, inhospitable dry lands set aside in what later became the state of Oklahoma. Many who could not keep up were left to die by the road as the U.S. Army marched the tribes westward.

The Seminoles of Florida were to be included in this forced exodus, but many refused to go. A series of broken promises by the U.S. government and threats to return the African Americans among them to slavery led to resistance, and then to a bloody armed uprising known as the Second Seminole War, which lasted from 1835 to 1842. Through visits to exhibits like those at Fort Christmas, visitors can learn about great Seminole resistance leaders like Osceola. The Seminoles sought to preserve their homeland; their African allies fought against reenslavement on the plantations of Alabama, Georgia, and South Carolina.

The Second Seminole War started at the Dade Battlefield (a site described in this guidebook) on December 28, 1835, and ended with the defeat or capture of most of the Seminole forces in 1842. Others retreated into the lands south of a line due east of Tampa. An uneasy peace prevailed, with the unmapped and unexplored (by whites) land south of that line representing an informal reservation. Some of the Seminoles were rounded up, taken to Tampa Bay, then transported by ship to New Orleans, and by riverboat to Arkansas for the arduous overland march to barren lands in Oklahoma.

Sporadic violence led to the construction of a line of about fifteen forts across the state and down the Atlantic coast—now marked only by a site at Paynes Creek (Fort Chokonikla) and a set of place-names, but no remaining forts—that includes Fort Pierce, Jupiter, and Fort Lauderdale. In 1855–58, a shorter war, known as the Third Seminole War, or Billy Bowlegs' War, saw action at some of these forts. Displays and interpreters at Fort Christmas, Fort Foster, and Fort Cooper tell parts of the Second Seminole War and Billy Bowlegs' War stories.

Meanwhile, the United States began to build what came to be known as the Third System of Fortifications, designed to defend the United States from naval attack on strategic coastal points. In Florida, four of those forts have survived. The massive brick-and-mortar forts, with heavy guns pointed seaward, can be visited at Fort Clinch, at the most northeasterly corner of the state on Amelia Island; at Fort Zachary Taylor in Key West; at Fort Pickens and Barrancas defending Pensacola; and at the isolated and dramatic island Fort Jefferson, on Garden Key in the Dry Tortugas, accessible today by boat or seaplane from Key West. Ironically, even as these forts were being completed, fortification engineers realized that they were already outmoded by the development of exploding shells and heavier shipborne rifled cannon.

Despite their obsolescence, all of these forts played crucial roles in the American Civil War (1861–65), as the Union blockaded the seceding southern states to cut off imports and exports. Union troops held Fort Pickens, near Pensacola, one of three forts in the Confederate states (all in Florida) that never fell to Confederate troops. Dr. Samuel Mudd, implicated in the assassination of Lincoln, served a prison term at Fort Jefferson after the Civil War. President Andrew Johnson, in the last weeks of his administration, pardoned Mudd, partly for his heroic work with yellow-fever patients at his remote prison.

Union and Confederate troops fought a major battle in Florida near Lake City, at Olustee, a few miles to the east of that city, just off the modern-day I-10. No fort marks that spot, but a reenactment of the battle brings thousands of visitors annually. As Union troops occupied Fort Clinch on Amelia Island northeast of Jacksonville, a gun battle between a warship and a railroad train took place as a Union gunboat fired on the train carrying Confederates to safety. The Civil War historian Lewis Zerfas has

This Currier and Ives print of Fort Pickens was published in the 1860s. (Courtesy of the Library of Congress.)

noted this encounter as the first of its kind. That unique event is only one of dozens of "firsts" and unique events and precedents uncovered in the research for this guidebook. Another battle at Natural Bridge, just to the north of Fort San Marcos de Apalache, saw the Confederates defeat advancing Union forces, leaving Tallahassee as the only Confederate state capital east of the Mississippi that did not fall to the Union during that war.

In the mid-1880s, the War Department conducted a thorough study of America's fortifications in light of new developments in exploding shells and shipborne ordnance. The committee, headed by Secretary of War William Endicott, produced a comprehensive plan, known as the Endicott Plan, for modernizing the coastal forts. Although the government never implemented most of the plan, some improvements at Fort Zachary Taylor, at Fort Barrancas, and at Fort Pickens reflected new ideas about mounting fewer and more dispersed guns with longer range, and using concrete instead of bricks and mortar. These concrete "improvements," now deteriorating, can be found alongside the older and more rugged brickwork at all of these forts.

Some of these forts saw a minor revival during the Spanish-American War in 1898, with the addition of new guns to protect against a feared Spanish bombardment of coastal cities. Heavy guns were installed at Fort De Soto, at the entrance to Tampa Bay, as a result of that war, and guns were added in new batteries at Fort Zachary Taylor.

In the late nineteenth and early twentieth centuries, Florida became a tourist destination, offering its warm climate as a relief from the harsh winters of the Northeast. Among the many famous and creative Americans who wintered in Florida was the commander in chief, President Harry S. Truman, who established what was called the "Truman Little White House" in the former commandant's housing of the Key West naval base in the late 1940s. That site is included in this work because of its central significance in the military history of the United States: it was here that Truman and his advisors worked out the concept of a unified Department of Defense, combining the Navy and War Departments, in 1949. During World War II, the U.S. Army built one of the largest advanced training bases at Camp Blanding, due west of St. Augustine, just east of Starke, Florida. At its peak, Camp Blanding housed more people than all but three contemporary cities in Florida. A museum at Camp Blanding presents this story, still remembered by World War II veterans and their descendents.

Just as Florida had seen many coastal forts as part of the nation's defenses against sea attack, as the United States moved into the modern age of air combat, Florida hosted the construction of major airbases to protect the nation from attack by combined sea/air forces. The new facilities included the Pensacola Naval Air Station, Eglin Air Field, MacDill Air Force Base, and Tyndall Air Field, all of which remain active parts of the modern defense of the United States. Museums at two of these contemporary, twenty-first-century facilities draw thousands of visitors annually. For visitors who want deeper insights into the history of both the U.S. Air Force and the U.S. Navy Air Force, the Air Armament Museum at Eglin and the National Naval Air Museum at Pensacola are excellent places for learning. The bases where they are located continue the mission of protecting

On display at the Eglin Air Force Museum, near Fort Walton Beach, this U.S. Air Force jet is one of more than twenty-five aircraft on exhibit. The T-33 T-Bird was the pilot-trainer version of the Shooting Star widely used in the 1950s. The most widely used jet trainer in the world, nearly 7,000 were built. (Loretta Carlisle photo.)

the United States from possible foreign adversaries, now using twenty-first-century technology.

The entries in this guidebook are arranged by their location in the four regions of Florida: Northwest, Northeast, Central, and South. For visitors planning to stop by two or three forts on the same day on a tour, this grouping may be helpful. Mileages to nearby forts shown in most entries may help in planning such day trips.

If the reader of this guidebook prefers to use it as a reference to the military history of Florida, it may be better to read the entries in something approximating the chronological order usually found in history books. For such a reading, it would be appropriate to look at the entries for the forts in the following order:

Colonial era: Fort Caroline, Mission San Luis, Fort Mose, Fort Matanzas, Castillo de San Marcos;

Early nineteenth century and the Seminole Wars: Fort San Marcos de Apalache, Fort Gadsden, Fort Cooper, Dade Battlefield, Fort Christmas, Fort Foster, Fort Chokonikla (Paynes Creek);
Civil War period: Fort Barrancas, Fort Pickens, Fort Clinch, Fort Zachary Taylor, East and West Martello Towers, Fort Jefferson;
Spanish American War (1898), World War I, and early twentieth century: Fort De Soto;
World War II to the present: Camp Blanding, Truman Little White House, Air Force Armament Museum, and National Museum of Naval Aviation.

As a further aid in following the sequential history of Florida and its forts, a chronology provides the dates of wars, major battles in Florida, and the dates of establishment of the forts and their subsequent histories as historic sites for visitors.

Historic tourism in the United States, including visits to sites like those described in this book, has flourished in recent times. Figures show that the number of tourists visiting historic sites across the country every year runs in the millions. Considering what can be gained from such visits, this development is not at all surprising.

By visiting a historic site, standing in a location where great events transpired, and looking at ruins, structures, artifacts, period weapons, dioramas, replica buildings, and discussing history with curators, reenactors, and interpreters, parents and children can learn firsthand the startling, often rarely told stories of history. In Europe, Egypt, and the Holy Land, for centuries, tourists have visited the great sites of bygone eras; Americans, too, now recognize that a visit to their own battlefields, forts, and historic cities brings alive the rich past; Florida offers an array of venues to take us back hundreds of years into the rich stories of our past. Whether visitors are on a day trip or an extended tour, all of these sites will reward with new knowledge and new appreciation for the rich tapestry of American and Floridian History. Enjoy the trip, and take your camera!

1 Northwest Florida

The National Museum of Naval Aviation at Pensacola is the foremost museum of naval aircraft in the world. (Loretta Carlisle photo.)

1

National Museum of Naval Aviation

Location: On the Pensacola Naval Air Station at 1750 Radford Boulevard.
Driving Directions: From downtown Pensacola, follow Barrancas Avenue west to South Navy Boulevard. After crossing the bridge over Bayou Grande, bear right on Duncan Road, turn right at Taylor Avenue, and right at Radford Boulevard.
Hours of Operation: 9 a.m. to 5 p.m. daily. Closed Christmas, Thanksgiving, and New Year's Day.
Fees: No admission charge; charges vary for the IMAX theater and use of the flight simulators.
Phone: (850) 452-3604
Website: www.navalaviationmuseum.org

Unique Facts

The National Museum of Naval Aviation is one of the most visited museums in Florida; it is the largest museum of its kind in the world.

Things to See

Major attractions at the museum include an IMAX theater presentation of flight, flight simulators, and displays of vintage and modern naval aircraft. There are more than 150 carefully restored aircraft, numerous hands-on exhibits, and more than 4,000 artifacts from Navy, Marine Corps, and Coast Guard aviation. Call ahead to determine times for Blue Angels practice air shows from March through November. There is a motion-based Top Gun Air Combat simulator. The Flight Adventure Deck works closely with school groups to teach about gravity and flight. A self-guided tour can be downloaded from the website; organized guided tours leave at 11 a.m., 1 p.m., and 2:30 p.m. In addition, there is a 20-minute trolley tour of the outdoor aircraft. In order to reserve a seat on the trolley, guests should register at the main information desk just inside the museum entrance. The website contains detailed information on each of the aircraft on display.

The many aircraft on display include:

- NC-4 Flying Boat, the first aircraft to fly across the Atlantic. Contrary to popular impression, this two-man aircraft crossed the Atlantic fully seven years before "Lucky Lindy," Charles Lindbergh, made his solo flight to Paris.
- AV-8 Harrier "jump jet"
- SBD Dauntless from the Battle of Midway
- F-14 Tomcat, the last one to fly a combat mission
- A-4 Skyhawk as flown by the Blue Angels
- F-4N Phantom II, veteran of Vietnam War
- A-7 Corsair II from Desert Storm
- Apollo and Mercury space capsules

Things to See Nearby

Nearby military history sites in Florida include Fort Pickens and Fort Barrancas. Fort Barrancas is also on the Pensacola Naval Air Station, across Radford Avenue from the museum. A smaller Air Armament Museum, displaying Air Force planes and armaments, is located at Eglin Air Base. Eglin is about 58 miles east via I-10. The alternative route via US 98 is slower, taking well over an hour to reach Eglin.

History

Because of its strategic location, Pensacola has been the scene of forts, battles, and military engagements from early colonial times. In 1781, Spanish and French forces under Bernardo Gálvez attacked a British fort at Pensacola. During the attack, the fort's ammunition magazine detonated with a blast heard and seen from miles away.

Pensacola remained a strategic site from the eighteenth century through the twentieth and twenty-first centuries, with a navy yard and naval base constructed on the site of prior forts in the nineteenth century.

In the twentieth century, Pensacola Naval Air Base emerged as the anchor for the Navy's Air arm in the Gulf of Mexico. Naval aviation has played an important part in all of the wars fought by the United States since 1917. In 1921, U.S. Army Gen. Billy Mitchell demonstrated the effectiveness of aircraft bombing of warships, stimulating the further development of aircraft carriers. In World War II, the aircraft carrier and its planes bypassed the battleship as the mainstay of the Navy. Aircraft carriers could

View of Pensacola from Santa Rosa Island, engraved by Thomas Jeffrys and first published in London in 1768. (Courtesy of the Library of Congress.)

The USS *Iwo Jima* was the primary recovery ship for the astronauts aboard *Apollo 13*. (National Museum of Naval Aviation photo.)

project power by surprise strikes at enemy ships and land bases, covering hundreds of square miles with their presence. With the development of jet aircraft and intermediate-range cruise missiles, the reach of a carrier increased dramatically. As an instrument of national power, aircraft carriers have been at the beck and call of the president in crisis after crisis from 1945 to the present, placing American military might where needed around the world.

The Navy established the nation's first naval air station at Pensacola in 1914. The idea of establishing a museum to commemorate both Pensacola's role in naval air and the work of the Navy's air wing can be traced to Capt. Magruder H. Tuttle. He served at Pensacola in 1955 as chief of staff to the commander of Naval Air Basic Training. Tuttle suggested that a small museum could give young aviator trainees a sense of pride in their service and a knowledge of the history of naval air. However, he and his colleagues soon found out that funding for such a museum at the base would have to come out of the training command's regular budget. Several years later, Tuttle, now an admiral, returned to

Pensacola and revived the idea. This time, after working up the chain of command, the proposal received approval for funding through donations. The museum received formal approval in 1962 and opened June 8, 1963.

The museum had modest beginnings in a renovated wooden World War II building, with a display of eight aircraft, rotated through storage from spots located on the naval air station. The collection of older aircraft, many needing professional restoration, soon outgrew the small spaces allotted, and in 1964, the Chief of Naval Operations (CNO) supported further expansion through a nonprofit corporation. In 1966, the Naval Aviation Museum Association obtained 501(c)(3) nonprofit corporation status. With the funds raised, the association arranged with architects and builders for a new structure to house the collection.

Thinking ahead, planners worked on a modular approach that could be expanded as the number of aircraft and displays grew. The museum dedicated the $4 million Phase I 68,000-square-foot structure in 1975. Under the direction of Adm. Thomas Moorer, Retired CNO and chairman of the Joint Chiefs, the museum completed Phase II in 1980, bringing the capacity to 110,000 square

The Hoverfly helicopter was designed by Igor Sikorsky and first flew in 1942. (National Museum of Naval Aviation photo.)

feet. The museum finished Phase III in 1990, increasing the floor space to 250,000 square feet, with the modules connected by a 75-foot-high atrium. Restoration of recovered aircraft, some salvaged from Lake Michigan or sites in the Pacific, added to the unique displays at the facility, now in a special room denoted as "Sunken Treasures."

New emphasis on bringing history alive included dioramas and displays that helped carry visitors back to the World War II period, including the home front and the Pacific campaigns. In 1992, the facility added the Emil Buehler Naval Aviation Library for professional historical research into naval aviation, one of the most complete collections on the topic available in the world. The year 1994 saw Phase IIIa, including the IMAX theater and the production of an IMAX film, *The Magic of Flight*. The theater and associated facilities brought the museum's square footage to 291,000. The special atrium displays the Blue Angels demonstration jets. Separate displays are devoted to prisoner-of-war conditions, lighter-than-air aircraft, World War II aircraft carriers, Coast Guard aviation, and other topics.

The history of the museum is dramatic enough, but the history of naval aviation told through the IMAX film, the interactive displays and flight simulators, through artifacts, aircraft, and dioramas is compelling for visitors. Tourists as well as researchers find the careful restorations and the dozens of aircraft memorable and informative, bringing alive the role of naval air in the defense of the nation over more than seven decades.

2

Fort Barrancas

Location: On the Pensacola Naval Air Station ½ mile east of the Naval Air Museum, located on Taylor Road.
Driving Directions: From downtown Pensacola, take Barrancas Avenue (SR 292) east to U.S. Navy Boulevard south. After crossing the bridge over Bayou Grande, bear right on Duncan Road to Taylor Road. Turn right on Taylor Road and follow to Fort Barrancas. Before reaching Fort Barrancas, visitors will pass the Advanced Redoubt, off to the right on Taylor Road, which is well worth a separate stop.
Hours of Operation: Visitor center is open 9:30 a.m. to 4:45 p.m., March through October; 8:30 a.m. to 3:45 p.m., November through February.

Fort Barrancas ranger-guided tours (30 to 45 minutes) are given daily at 2 p.m. Advanced Redoubt ranger-guided tours (30 to 45 minutes) are given on Saturdays at 11 a.m.
Fees: No admission charge. The park is operated by the National Park Service as part of the Gulf Islands National Seashore.
Phone: (850) 455-5167

Special Events

Candlelight tours depart the visitor center every 15 minutes and last one hour. Saturdays, mid-January to mid-February, 5 p.m. to 7:15 p.m.

Unique Facts

A brief exchange of gunfire at Fort Barrancas between secessionist Florida troops and U.S. Army forces on January 8, 1861, can be considered the "first shots" of the Civil War, as they took place three months before the more famous engagement at Fort Sumter in Charleston harbor, South Carolina. Several features of the fort, including the scarp and counterscarp galleries, are unique.

Things to See

The fort has many aspects of the Third System of Fortifications, some of which are unique to this fort. Among the features to be observed are the glacis, or earthen slope, that hides the fort from land-based artillery. The main walls, or scarp, are 20 feet high and 4 feet thick; the outer walls, or counterscarp, contain cannon that could be fired down the moat or ditch. A drawbridge, operated by counterweight and winch, pivots at the center. The brief gunfire exchange in January 1861 that predated Fort Sumter took place at the drawbridge.

Shots fired at this drawbridge in January 1861 preceded the firing on Fort Sumter and are regarded by some as the first shots of the U.S. Civil War. (Loretta Carlisle photo.)

The original Spanish architectural detail is seen above the doors at the water battery at Fort Barrancas. (Loretta Carlisle photo.)

The scarp gallery is a series of arches that support the sand fill and have loopholes for firing muskets. Vents in the ceiling allowed the escape of smoke from firing weapons. A tunnel or gallery under the ditch leads out to the counterscarp gallery, which contained cannon emplacements and powder magazines. At one time, a shot furnace stood in the center of the fort parade ground, a spot now marked only by a brick foundation. Another long, sloping tunnel leads out to the water battery, originally constructed by the Spanish as Bateria de San Antonio. Guns mounted in the water battery fired straight across the level of the harbor at hostile ships, and the original water battery at this location had been built long prior to U.S. occupation.

Things to See Nearby

A short distance from Fort Barrancas is the Naval Air Museum. The "Advanced Redoubt" is available for a visit via a ½-mile walk along the marked "Trench Trail," or by a short drive back on Taylor Road. A trip out to Santa Rosa Island will take the visitor to

Fort Pickens, a companion fort also designed to guard Pensacola harbor.

History

The British built the first fort on this location in 1763, during their short period of occupation of Florida, locating it to protect the town of Pensacola. Bernardo de Gálvez sailed past the fort in 1781 to take possession of Pensacola for Spain at the end of the American Revolution. Spain had joined forces with the American Patriots in the American War for Independence in 1779. At that time, Gálvez, governor of Spanish Louisiana, began planning a campaign to take over British West Florida. In late 1779, his forces took control of the lower Mississippi River and obtained the surrender of British forces at the Battle of Baton Rouge. He captured Mobile on March 14, 1780, after a siege. Gálvez planned to attack Pensacola, West Florida's capital, using Spanish troops from Havana, and using Mobile as the base for attack. British troops reinforced Pensacola in April 1780, setting back Gálvez's plans; a hurricane led to a further setback in October 1780. Gálvez regrouped his fleet at Havana.

At Pensacola, after the outbreak of hostilities with Spain in 1779, British Gen. John Campbell began construction of additional defenses. By early 1781, the Pensacola garrison consisted of a mix of troops, including Loyalists from Maryland and Pennsylvania, and Native American troops from the Creek Nation. Pensacola had an earthwork fort with a palisade, called Fort George, strengthened by Campbell. He also built two redoubts in 1780 to the north and northwest of Fort George, and a battery of guns at what later became Fort Barrancas.

Gálvez led his forces, about 1,300 strong, aboard a Spanish fleet from Havana on February 13, 1781. Furthermore, he ordered additional troops from New Orleans and Mobile. He landed troops on Santa Rosa Island and emplaced artillery there to drive out British ships in the bay. His ships were too deeply laden to enter the bay, and British guns from shore held them off.

A lucky shot from advancing Spanish troops detonated a British powder magazine in Pensacola, as depicted in this 1784 drawing by Nicolas Ponce. (Courtesy of the Library of Congress.)

Using commercial ships from Louisiana, he sailed past the British guns into the bay. As Gálvez maneuvered his troops ashore, reinforcements arrived from Cuba, bringing more Spanish and French troops. With the strengthened forces, he laid siege to the British position in Pensacola.

On May 5, 1781, Spanish cannons found the mark when they hit the magazine in one of the British redoubts. The explosion killed an estimated eighty-five men and left the fort in ruins. The Spanish quickly occupied the position and began using it to shell Fort George itself. At 3:00 p.m., the fort's garrison raised the white flag. The surrender included the entirety of British West Florida. Gálvez had the guns, and Fort Barrancas Coloradas moved closer to the entrance to the bay.

The Spanish rebuilt the fort, naming it San Carlos de Barrancas. The Spanish began work on the water battery in 1793 and completed it in 1797. In Spanish, a *barranca* is a bluff or cliff. To protect the water battery from the rear, the Spanish constructed a long palisade, mounting some twenty-three cannons.

The moat surrounding the Advanced Redoubt was part of the extensive, land-side protection of Fort Barrancas. (Loretta Carlisle photo.)

Nothing remains of the British position "Fort George" in Pensacola. However, a small re-created part of the fort marks its original location. Visitors can see this reconstruction as part of the Fort George Memorial Park, in the North Hill Preservation District. The park is located on La Rua and Palafox Streets in Pensacola. The U.S. National Register of Historic Places added the reconstructed palisade and emplacement to its register on July 8, 1974.

On his way to defeat the British at New Orleans in 1814, Andrew Jackson crossed into the Spanish territory of Florida in pursuit of British troops. As he approached Pensacola, the British evacuated, burning the Spanish fort and spiking the guns to render them useless. In 1818, Jackson returned during the First Seminole War and captured both Pensacola and the forts there. Neither President James Monroe nor Congress supported Jackson's invasion, and he withdrew. Spain finally ceded the territory of Florida to the United States in 1821.

When the United States acquired Florida from Spain in 1821 under the Adams-Onis Treaty, the U.S. government began to fortify the seaports of Florida to protect them from invasion under the Third System of Fortifications. The Navy built a naval shipyard in Pensacola, and the Army constructed four forts, beginning in 1829, to protect the navy yard and Pensacola harbor: Fort McRee on Foster's Bank or Perdido Island; Fort Pickens at the westernmost tip of Santa Rosa Island; Fort Barrancas and the Advanced Redoubt on the mainland near the navy yard. The Advanced Redoubt served the sole purpose of protecting Fort Barrancas from a land attack, but the Union army had stationed no additional troops there on the eve of the Florida militia attack in January 1861.

Fort Barrancas incorporated the existing Spanish works, which consisted of a water battery designed to fire at sea level straight at incoming enemy ships. Joseph Totten, the lead engineer of the Army Corps of Engineers (for whom the Totten shutters found at Fort Jefferson were named), designed Fort Barrancas. Maj. (later Col.) William H. Chase managed the actual construction work. He contracted with local slaveholders for slave labor and with local brickyards for an estimated 6 million bricks.

In January 1861, U.S. Army forces and Florida militia confronted each other at the drawbridge. The troops loyal to the Union fired a few shots, but the muskets may have been loaded with powder only. As a result, it has been argued, this was not really the "first shot" of the Civil War. Nevertheless, the standoff closely resembled conditions in Charleston harbor that led to the evacuation of Fort Moultrie and the occupation of Fort Sumter. In Pensacola, Lt. Adam Slemmer led the troops from Fort Barrancas out to occupy and hold Fort Pickens. Fort Pickens remained in Union hands throughout the Civil War, although state

GENERAL BRAGG'S CAMP, AS SEEN FROM FORT PICKENS.—[Drawn by an Officer of the Fort.]

OUR ILLUSTRATIONS OF FORT PICKENS.

We publish on page 374, from a sketch by an officer in Fort Pickens, a view of a Mortar Battery lately erected on Santa Rosa Island by the Federal troops, and on this page a View of General Bragg's Camp, from a drawing by the same officer, and a drawing of the interior of one of the Sand-bag Batteries bearing on Fort Pickens, from a sketch by our artist who has been traveling with W. H. Russell, Esq., LL.D., Correspondent of the London *Times*.

The officer to whom we are indebted for the two first-mentioned pictures thus writes us concerning them:

Fort Pickens, *May* 11, 1861.

With this you will receive a sketch of part of one of the Federal Mortar Batteries on Santa Rosa Island, near Fort Pickens.

This battery, a portion of which is seen in the sketch, was recently built by Lieutenant Tidball, of the 2d Artillery. The central object in the view is a bomb-proof shelter, used as a retreat from a heavy fire, the mass of sand on its roof forming a perfect security against shells of the largest calibre. The powder and loaded shells are kept in similar shelters, according to the usage of war. The ruin of brick-work on its left, and but a few feet in its rear, is all that remains of a large redoubt once held by the English. Whether they built it or no I can not tell, as in those days there was a proverb that the "Spanish built forts, the English held them, and the French took them." When General Jackson came down to Pensacola in 1814, to look after Federal interests in his unauthorized but energetic way, he found the Spanish occupying several points about the place, all protected by a net-work of friendly relations with the Home Secretary in England, who was well represented on the occasion by a fine body of English troops fresh from the Peninsula. A portion of these occupied the redoubt whose ruins are seen in the sketch. Jackson cut the net-work by opening fire without orders—an example that might be followed with advantage by some Federalists of the present day. The Spanish and English withdrew after blowing up the forts and redoubts. In 1819 they returned again, but again the Federalists ousted them. It is a curious coincidence that our Government should occupy these points immortalized in history—that it should be here building up new works to teach its rebellious children a lesson that they might have learned on the site of the old. I looked with curious feeling upon some old nine-pound shot that the workmen turned up the other day while building the battery. Those shot were fired by Jackson, in all probability, and answered by some long "thirty-twos," which now lie on some old logs at the left of the battery. Many years have rolled by since their hoarse voices were heard by Jackson as he threw off the dead weight of official ignorance and drove the intruders from Florida. You can still see the big "G. R." on the reinforce of the guns, but time has strewn huge scales from their muzzles amidst the grass where they have lain neglected so long.

This battery is only a part of the defences outside of the fort. This side of it the ground rolls off in a series of sand hills, which form excellent natural traverses, and would well conceal from the enemy as many as ten or fifteen regiments.

In sending us the view of General Bragg's camp, he says:

Fort Pickens, *May* 12, 1861.

Inclosed I send you a sketch of the encampment west of the light-house and nearly opposite Fort Pickens. In front of the tents, near the shore, is seen one of their sand batteries, in which they have mounted several Columbiads. It is reported that they have now 10,000 men here; but I imagine 6000 is much nearer the exact number. This battery commands the entrance to the harbor, but is too far off to do much injury to the fort, the distance being nearly 1½ miles. The light-house seen on the right is a very fine one, but has not been lighted since the night of April 12, when it was suddenly extinguished during a great scare of the secessionists, caused by the firing of a few guns from the *Wyandotte*, which led them to suspect the fleet was coming in. They immediately extinguished the light and lighted up their batteries. In the mean time, Captain Vodges's company landed, captured one of their guard-boats, which, as soon as the troops were in the fort, was allowed to go back, and convey to General Bragg the gratifying intelligence that the fort was reinforced.

COLONEL MOREHEAD'S CAMP AT BALTIMORE.

We publish on page 374 a View of the Encampment of United States Volunteers, under Colonel Morehead, on the land adjoining Patterson's Park, Baltimore. Patterson's Park will be seen on the left of the tents in the picture. If the late accounts from Baltimore be correct, this encampment will possess remarkable interest before long.

INTERIOR OF A SAND-BAG BATTERY AT PENSACOLA BEARING ON FORT PICKENS.—[Sketched by our Artist, who has been traveling with W. H. Russell, LL.D., Barrister at Law.]

Union forces set up a large camp outside Fort Pickens to protect it from Confederate attack. Pictured in *Harper's Weekly*, the June 1861 encampment here would face a major battle in October. (Courtesy of the Library of Congress.)

troops moved into Barrancas, the Advanced Redoubt, and Fort McRee. (In some early publications, Fort McRee is spelled "Fort McRae.") During heavy gun battles in November 1861 and January 1862, gunfire almost completely destroyed Fort McRee, but Pickens remained undefeated. Colonel Chase, who had overseen the construction of both Barrancas and Pickens, led the Florida militia's effort to defeat the Union stronghold at Fort Pickens. Union ships blockading the port of Pensacola sometimes fired their cannon in salute of the Union outpost at Fort Pickens.

Under the Endicott Plan developed in the mid-1880s, the War Department supplied Fort Barrancas with new guns in 1894. New concrete fortifications built under the new plan at Pickens and McRee rendered Barrancas obsolete as a fort in 1896, but it continued to be used as a small-arms range and then as a storage facility. The Army turned the forts over to the Navy in 1946, and Fort Barrancas became part of the Gulf Islands National Seashore in 1971. The fort opened to the public after restoration by the National Park Service in 1980.

This depiction of the USS *Wyandotte* firing a salute to Fort Barrancas was published in 1861 in *Harper's Weekly*. Fort Barrancas is on the left in the background. (Courtesy of the Library of Congress.)

In this *Harper's Weekly* illustration of December 1861, Fort McRee is visible on the left, Fort Pickens in the foreground, and Fort Barrancas, in Confederate control, in the background. (Courtesy of the Library of Congress.)

Virtually nothing remains to be seen at the site of Fort McRee, which is inaccessible by vehicle and can be reached only by a long sand-hike or by boat at the eastern tip of Perdido Key. The actual foundations of Fort McRee are now submerged, as the barrier islands are gradually moving to the West. Only a few concrete foundations of later gun emplacements at Batteries 233, Slemmer, and Center can be seen ashore.

3

Fort Pickens

Location: In the Gulf Islands National Seashore, on the Gulf of Mexico, at the westernmost end of Santa Rosa Island, guarding the entrance to Pensacola Bay.
Driving Directions: From Pensacola, take US 98 (Gulf Breeze Parkway) south across the toll bridge to CR 399 to Pensacola Beach. At Fort Pickens Road, turn right into Gulf Islands National Seashore. The fort is about 9.5 miles due west on Fort Pickens Road.
Hours of Operation: 7 a.m. until dusk, daily. Closed Christmas. The visitor center is open 9:30 a.m. to 4:45 p.m., March to October; 8:30 a.m. to 3:45 p.m., November to February.
Fees: $8 per vehicle to enter the park; no charge to tour the fort.
Phone: (850) 934-2600 (National Park Service, Florida information)
Note: Storms have closed the access road to Fort Pickens from time to time, so it is advisable to verify that the beach road is open for vehicles. Blowing sand is regularly plowed from the road, but take care not to veer off into the soft sandy shoulders or dunes.

Unique Facts

Fort Pickens was one of only three forts in the states that seceded from the Union that remained in Union hands throughout the Civil War. In addition, neither Fort Jefferson nor Fort Zachary Taylor, also in Florida, ever surrendered to the Confederacy.

The reverse arch shown here at Fort Pickens is an unusual architectural feature allowing support in a sandy base for the heavy masonry walls above. (Loretta Carlisle photo.)

Four forts originally protected Pensacola harbor: Fort Pickens, Fort Barrancas, the Advanced Redoubt at Barrancas, and Fort McRee (now vanished). Pickens has an excellent example of a "reverse arch," showing how archways constructed in sand were supported by an upside-down arch embedded in the soft surface.

Things to See

Although damaged by storms and a devastating magazine explosion, the fort walls, casemates, and parade ground are all open for visiting and are well worth the visit. A visitor center at Fort Pickens provides sheets for self-guided tours as well as a short video describing the fort.

Things to See Nearby

Nearby sites of military interest include Fort Barrancas at the Pensacola Naval Air Station. The visitor center there includes information about Fort Pickens. The Pensacola Naval Air Museum is also located at the Pensacola Naval Air Station. Eglin Air Force Base is about 55 miles due east on CR 399 and US 98.

History

Fort Pickens served as part of the Third System of Fortifications following the War of 1812. The French military engineer Baron Simon Bernard (who had been appointed as a U.S. Army brigadier general) designed the fort, and laborers built it over a five-year period, 1829–34. More than 21 million bricks went into the fort's construction, a quantity larger than that used for Fort Jefferson. However, since weather and explosion have destroyed much of Fort Pickens, Fort Jefferson remains the largest brick structure in the United States.

Fort Pickens lies at the extreme western end of Santa Rosa Island, situated to protect the entrance to the harbor and to control the island itself from land invasion. On a map, it is easy to see that Pickens and McRee guarded the passage into the harbor, while Barrancas guarded the mainland approaches to the city itself.

Col. William H. Chase of the Army Corps of Engineers supervised the construction work at Fort Pickens. (One of the main streets of Pensacola is named for him.) During the Civil War, Chase resigned his U.S. Army commission and joined the secession forces. There is some irony in the fact that, as the builder of the fort, he led Florida's effort to capture the fort for the Florida militia.

In 1860, Fort Pickens had been abandoned since 1848 and had fallen into disrepair. In an action very similar to the more famous occupation of Fort Sumter in the harbor of Charleston, South Carolina, U.S. army troops abandoned a shore facility and occupied the more defensible offshore fort. Although Lt. Robert

The burning of the dry dock at the navy yard in Pensacola, April 1861, was clearly visible from Fort Pickens, as shown in this *Harper's Weekly* illustration. (Courtesy of the Library of Congress.)

Anderson, who led the evacuation of Fort Moultrie and the occupation of Fort Sumter, became a national hero for the Union, his counterpart in Florida never earned such fame. Lt. Adam J. Slemmer commanded the U.S. forces at Fort Barrancas. On January 8, 1861 (fully three months before the "official" start of the Civil War with the firing on Fort Sumter), Florida secessionists attacked Slemmer's small command. The fort's guards repelled the attack after a short skirmish. Slemmer then ordered some 20,000 pounds of gunpowder at Barrancas destroyed, and had the guns spiked. Then Slemmer, with some eighty loyal Union troops, evacuated Barrancas and moved to Fort Pickens, which remained in Union hands throughout the Civil War.

In August 1861, Union troops set fire to a large dry dock at the Pensacola Navy Yard, then in Confederate hands. The huge fire could be seen clearly by the Union troops out at Fort Pickens.

The Confederate Gen. Braxton Bragg led efforts to subdue Fort Pickens. On October 9, 1861, Confederate forces unsuccessfully tried to take the fort from the shore side in the Battle of Santa Rosa Island. Advancing Confederates surprised the Sixth

Harper's Weekly published these different sketches of life at Fort Pickens by U.S. Army officers on duty there in 1861. (Courtesy of the Library of Congress.)

"The Battle of Santa Rosa Island, October 9, 1861—the attack upon Wilson's Camp" by Charles Allgouer. (Engraving in *Harper's Weekly*, December 1861. Courtesy of the Library of Congress.)

Infantry regiment of New York Volunteers encamped outside the walls of the fort, and a sharp battle ensued with casualties on both sides. A massive artillery duel on November 22, 1861, between Union ships and the Union forces at Fort Pickens on one side and the shore batteries on the other side, resulted in heavy damage to Confederate-held Fort McRee.

General Bragg reported that the exchange of gunfire was the heaviest artillery battle to date in the history of the world. He may have been right. Forts Pickens, Jefferson, and Zachary Taylor—three Florida Third System Forts—were held by Union forces and played crucial parts in the Union blockade of Florida.

From 1886 to May 1887, the U.S. government imprisoned Chiricahua Apache Indian leader Geronimo in Fort Pickens, along with several others. Meanwhile, the government held their families as prisoners at Castillo de San Marcos in St. Augustine, then known as Fort Marion. In the summer of 1887, the government relocated them all to less austere but still unhealthy imprisonment at Mount Vernon barracks in Alabama.

Artillery added at Fort Pickens after the Civil War was never fired in battle. (Loretta Carlisle photo.)

The staircase to the upper ramparts of Fort Pickens, like the walls themselves, reflect the brick mason's art. (Loretta Carlisle photo.)

An accidental detonation of stored gunpowder in 1899 sent bricks across the bay as far as Pensacola. The damaged corner bastion was never repaired. (Loretta Carlisle photo.)

New gun batteries were constructed at Fort Pickens in the 1880s and 1890s. Following a plan developed by the Endicott Board (convened by Secretary of War William Endicott), crews installed fewer and more dispersed modern guns. Under this plan, they built Battery Pensacola within the walls of Fort Pickens, and constructed similar concrete batteries to the east and west as separate facilities. The ruins of these later facilities can still be seen on the island.

A fire on June 20, 1899, in Bastion D of Fort Pickens reached the magazine, and set off 8,000 pounds of powder. The damage from the blast left one side of the fort open, and the unrepaired damaged arches still provide testimony to the massive detonation. The explosion killed one soldier, Pvt. Earle F. Welles, and destroyed Bastion D. Some of the bricks from the magazine flew across the harbor, landing at the Pensacola Naval Station.

Concrete batteries added to the fort complex include Battery Pensacola (inside the fort itself in 1899 and abandoned in 1934); Batteries Cullum, Sevier, and Van Swearingen in 1898, just to the west of the fort but closed to visitors; and Battery Payne in

1904 and Battery Trueman in 1905 at the westernmost tip of the island. On the drive into or away from the main fort, the concrete Battery Worth (1899) is just to the north of the road and has a picnic area. Other batteries can be accessed by well-marked side roads and trails: Battery 234 (1934), a World War II Tower; Battery Cooper (1906); Battery GPF (1937); and Battery Langdon (built in 1923 and casemated in 1943).

By the end of World War II, advances in weaponry made the fortress completely outdated. The last artilleryman left Fort Pickens in 1947. Through the 1950s and 1960s, the Florida State Park Service administered Fort Pickens, but the state could afford only minimal maintenance. In 1972, the fort and its surrounding area became a unit in the newly established Gulf Islands National Seashore. Following extensive research and repairs by the National Park Service, the Service reopened the fort to the public in 1976. The Park Service installed two 8-inch Rodman guns (for exhibit purposes) on top of the Tower Bastion at the west side of the fort, accessible by staircases. From time to time, storms have destroyed the access road to the fort, as with hurricanes Dennis and Katrina in 2005; although as of 2011, crews have kept the fort road open for visitors.

4

Air Force Armament Museum

Location: At the Eglin Air Force Base, Niceville.
Driving Directions: From I-10, take exit 56 to SR 85 South, about 19 miles. Follow signs toward Eglin Air Force Base and the Air Force Armament Museum.
Hours of Operation: 9:30 a.m. to 4:30 p.m. (Central Standard Time), Monday through Saturday. Closed Sunday and federal holidays. Visitors driving from eastern Florida should recognize the change of time zone from Eastern to Central (an hour earlier) just west of exit 66 on I-10.
Fees: No admission charge; donations accepted.
Phone: (850) 882-4062

Unique Facts

The museum has the largest display of U.S. Air Force aircraft and armaments outside the National Air Force Museum at the Wright-Patterson Air Field in Ohio.

Things to See

There are twenty-five aircraft on display outdoors, and visitors are welcome to walk through the display area. Each aircraft has a plaque that describes the aircraft, its period of production, its armament and function, along with other details of the specific airplane. The spacious grounds allow expansion with new acquisitions, and the number of aircraft changes from time to time. Inside the museum are four aircraft on display, each representing a specific war era: the P-51 Mustang and the P-47, both from World War II; the F-80 Shooting Star, from the Korean War era, and the F-105 Thunderchief from the Vietnam War.

A "gun vault" contains a range of weapons from the 1903 Springfield rifle to the modern GAU-8, which can fire up to 6,000 rounds per minute. Further detail on the displays is found below.

Things to See Nearby

The National Museum of Naval Aviation in Pensacola is about an hour and a half drive west via I-10. Smaller outdoor displays of aircraft can also be seen at Hurlburt Field (20 miles west via SR 85 and US 98) and at Tyndall Air Force Base (about 75 miles east on US 98).

History and Detail of Displays

The Air Armament Museum grew out of a small program at Eglin Air Force Base in the 1970s. After an extensive fund-raising effort, and with support from Congressman Robert Sikes, the museum officially opened in 1985. Operating on a small budget, the museum has mounted an extensive and informative display of U.S. Air Force aircraft. The small scale of the museum, its friendly staff of volunteers, and the opportunity it offers visitors to view aircraft from all angles, on foot, make a visit unique and rewarding.

On display outside are examples of the famous "spy plane," the SR-71 Blackbird. Other aircraft include the A-10 Thunderbolt, B-17, C-47 Spooky, F-15 Eagle, F-16 Fighting Falcon, and a Soviet MIG-21. The largest aircraft are on the grounds in front of the museum, including a B-52 bomber, the SR-71, a World War II–vintage B-25, a B-17, the B-57 Canberra, and the Lockheed AC-130 gunship.

At the Air Force Armament Museum, this Soviet-built MiG-21 Fishbed was a short-range fighter-interceptor and the first production version of the aircraft. The term "MiG" represented the initials of the Soviet airplane design bureau founded by Artem Mikoyan and Mikhail Gurevich. (Loretta Carlisle photo.)

Among the many aircraft on display at the Air Force Armament Museum is this F-111 Aardvark, a medium-range interdictor and tactical strike aircraft that also served as a strategic bomber, reconnaissance, and electronic warfare airplane in various models. It first was deployed in 1967 and the U.S. Air Force versions officially retired by 1998. (Loretta Carlisle photo.)

The Lockheed F-104 Starfighter was a high-performance, supersonic interceptor that served with the U.S. Air Force from 1958 until 1969. (Loretta Carlisle photo.)

The panels with each outdoor aircraft give excellent details. For example, regarding the F-111 Aardvark, the outdoor plaque contains not only information about the armament and specifications of the aircraft, but the missions flown in Libya in 1986, in Desert Storm in Iraq in 1991, and in Bosnia in 1995.

Each of the planes in the outdoor display has a similarly detailed plaque, giving technical specifications as well as the general history of the aircraft, and the history of the particular plane on display. Technical specifications include thrust, length, height, wingspan, weight, speed, range, ceiling, and armament, if any. The T-33 T-Bird, for example, served as a training aircraft for pilots already qualified to fly propeller-driven aircraft, lengthened from the F-80 model to accommodate a second cockpit. As a training aircraft, the T-33 did not carry armament. Other aircraft on display include the F-104 Starfighter and the RF-4 Phantom II.

Armament on display inside the museum include the MOAB (Massive Ordnance Air Blast), nicknamed the "Mother of All

The RF-4 Phantom was a version of the F-4 jet fighter employed during the Vietnam War. The F-4 jet saw service with the Air Force, Marines, and Navy beginning in 1960. The last F-4 on active service was retired in 2004. (Loretta Carlisle photo.)

Bombs" because it is the largest "conventional" (non-nuclear) bomb in the U.S. arsenal. Other missiles are the Paveway series, the Falcons, Tomahawk, Mace, and Hound Dog. So-called "iron" bombs—that is, nonguided general-purpose bombs—are also on display. Full-scale models include "Fat Man," the nuclear weapon detonated over Nagasaki, Japan, in 1945, and the GBU-28 "bunker buster" developed for use during Desert Storm.

A 32-minute film, *Arming the Air Force*, is shown in the museum's theater continuously throughout the day. The museum has two large murals donated by artist Mickey Harris of Crestview, Florida. A series of panels shows the role of the Air Force in numerous operations since the 1980s, including Operation Just Cause (1989–90) in Panama; Desert Storm (1990–91) in Iraq; Provide Promise (1992–96) in Bosnia; Southern and Northern Watch in Iraq through 2003; Noble Eagle 2001–Present (Homeland Security in the United States); Enduring Freedom (2001–11) Afghanistan; and Iraqi Freedom, 2003–11.

Other panels and dioramas give information about the history of Eglin Air Force Base, information about weapon systems, and details of Air Force history from its earliest days with the vigorous advocacy of Gen. Billy Mitchell, through the vital role of the Air Force in America's wars of the twentieth and twenty-first centuries.

The museum is funded by a foundation, the Air Force Armament Museum Foundation (AFAMF), a nonprofit organization established for the sole purpose of building the museum and seeing to its continued growth. The foundation operates the gift shop, which sells books, souvenirs, and Air Force–related gifts. The museum staff is supplemented by volunteers who serve not only in visitor liaison but work in aircraft restoration and maintenance. The small paid staff is headed by Lt. Col. (Ret) George Jones.

5

Fort Gadsden ("The Negro Fort")

Location: Near Sumatra, in the Apalachicola National Forest.
Driving Directions: From Tallahassee, take SR 20 west to Hasford; turn left on SR 65. Follow SR 65 into Franklin County. Watch for sign indicating turnoff to Fort Gadsden Historic Site. Turn right onto Forest Road 129-B toward Fort Gadsden. The fort site is in an isolated location, more than a mile from the highway on a maintained dirt road.
Hours of Operation: Daily until sundown.
Fees: No admission charge.
Phone: (850) 670-8616. School groups and others may arrange for an interpretive presentation.

Unique Facts

The site saw the largest battle in history between fugitive slaves and U.S. forces seeking to reenslave them.

Things to See

Nothing remains of the fort except the rubble from the fort's stone walls, leaving an outline of the fort and parade ground next to the Apalachicola River. A short interpretive trail leads visitors around the site. An ill-defined depression in the ground marks the moat of the original British fort. A small shelter contains

All that remains of Fort Gadsden is the earthen outline of the fort grounds, haunted by the spirits of those who died there. (Loretta Carlisle photo.)

displays explaining the history of the forts located there. The isolation of the spot, the tragic military history of the location, and the haunting cries of birds in the trees add up to offer a unique and rather impressive experience.

Things to See Nearby

Nearby military history sites include Fort San Marcos de Apalache, south of Tallahassee, and Mission San Luis in Tallahassee. However, the site of Fort Gadsden is extremely isolated, and the long ride to and from it will preclude combining this visit with another for most visitors.

History

Although little remains of the original forts at the site, the location is particularly rich in some of the little-known aspects of the

At the site of the ruins of Fort Gadsden, an information kiosk provides historical details. (Loretta Carlisle photo.)

history of Florida, and in the struggle against slavery by African Americans. The information kiosk at the site helps inform visitors of the fort's unique history.

During the War of 1812, the British sought to recruit Red Stick Creeks and fugitive African American slaves as allies in the war against the United States. In August 1814, a force of more than one hundred officers and men under the command of British Marine Lt. Col. Edward Nicolls marched into the Apalachicola River region in Spanish West Florida. Nicolls and his troops recruited, trained, and equipped local Indians and many fugitive slaves or "Afro-Seminoles." Before Nicolls could accomplish very much, the war ended. The troops under his command had constructed a fort at this site, located at Prospect Bluff, some 15 miles north of the mouth of the Apalachicola River, and about 60 miles south of the ill-defined border with the United States. This fort, simply called "Prospect Bluff" or "the British Post," served as an outpost and a recruiting point for a "Corps of Colonial Marines" recruited by Nicolls from among fugitive slaves. Many African Americans had fought in the South on the British, or Loyalist, side during the American Revolution, and Nicolls hoped to build a resistance force against the United States in a similar fashion in this second British-American war.

When Nicolls and his British troops evacuated in the spring of 1815, they left behind the fully equipped fort and a force of about three hundred fugitive slaves that included some trained members of the Corps of Colonial Marines. With gunpowder, cannons, muskets, and some basic training in European fighting skills, they were a formidable force. In addition, some thirty Choctaw and Seminole recruits remained at the fort.

The fort became widely known, both to slaves and to the American defenders of slavery. As word of the Negro Fort spread through western Florida and north into Georgia and Alabama (and as far north as Tennessee and as far west as Mississippi), hundreds more freedom-seeking fugitive slaves headed for the remote location. By some estimates, as many as eight hundred fugitive slaves (including children) rapidly settled under the protection of the fort in the nearby region. The proslavery press in the United States expressed outrage about the presence of the threat just over the border in Spanish territory.

An African American leader by the name of Garçon and a Choctaw leader began conducting raids across the border into Georgia. The name of the Choctaw leader is not recorded.

Partly in response to this threat and to guard the Spanish-U.S. border, the U.S. Army built Fort Scott on the Flint River in Georgia. The overland route of supply to Fort Scott was a difficult one, and Gen. Andrew Jackson sought to supply the U.S. fort by a water route, with ships sailing up the Apalachicola River from the Gulf through the Spanish territory. Critics and later historians saw his plan as provocative—an intentional effort to provide an excuse for subduing the threat posed by the Negro Fort. A naval force tried to make the voyage up the river on July 17, 1816, but turned back under gunfire from the Negro Fort that killed four Americans. The incident served as all the "provocation" that General Jackson needed.

On July 27, Jackson ordered Brig. Gen. Edmund P. Gaines at Fort Scott to launch an expedition to destroy the Negro Fort. The

American forces included Creek Indian allies from Coweta. They were told that they could keep whatever weapons or goods they captured from the fort. Following a series of skirmishes, Lt. Col. Duncan Clinch led the American forces and their Creek allies in a heavy ground assault on the fort, supported by naval ships that came up the river under the command of Sailing Master Jarius Loomis.

The two sides exchanged cannon fire, but one of the first "hot shots" (a red-hot cannonball) fired by the U.S. forces penetrated the fort's powder magazine, setting off an explosion that killed some 270 of the fort's 300 occupants. Garçon and the Choctaw leader both survived and were captured, and both were executed. The handful of other survivors were sent back into slavery.

Despite the destruction at the fort, the American Creek allies salvaged hundreds of usable weapons from the ruins, giving them a powerful advantage over the Red Stick Creeks. The continuing conflict between the Creeks and U.S. troops, and the Seminoles and the Red Stick Creeks who had joined with the Seminoles became known as the First Seminole War. Spain, weakened by revolutions and uprisings throughout its empire in the New World, could do little more than protest the invasion of its territory by U.S. forces, nor could Spain bring any order to the lawless West Florida province.

Even though Florida remained under Spanish jurisdiction, Jackson, on his own authority, directed Lt. James Gadsden to rebuild the destroyed fort. He built it slightly to the south of the original location, as shown on contemporary maps. Jackson rewarded Gadsden by naming the fort after him. Two years later, in 1818, Jackson personally led another expedition against Fort San Marcos de Apalache (or Fort St. Marks) a bit to the east of Fort Gadsden. See the next entry for a description of the events at Fort San Marcos de Apalache.

One of the U.S. soldiers, Duncan McKrimmon, while stationed at Fort Gadsden, went fishing in the river and became lost. Seminoles acting under the direction of the prophet and leader "Francis" captured McKrimmon and planned to execute

These rusting remains of a river steamer are thought to be from the engine of the *Irvington,* which sank about four miles from the fort in 1838. (Loretta Carlisle photo.)

him in retaliation for the loss of a family member at Fowltown, in keeping with Creek and Seminole custom. However, in a tale that resembles that of Capt. John Smith and Pocahontas, Francis's daughter, Malee (anglicized later to "Milly"), begged that McKrimmon be spared. As a consequence, Francis sold McKrimmon to the Spanish, who immediately released him. In 1818, Jackson's troops captured Francis and executed him, but his family, including Milly, survived. Hearing of their capture, Duncan McKrimmon traveled to Fort Gadsden and offered to marry Milly, but she refused the offer. She had gone west in the U.S. government's Indian removal, and searchers later discovered her living in poverty on the Arkansas River. Despite efforts to grant her a small pension for her role in saving McKrimmon's life, she passed away in 1848 before the measure could be approved. A plaque describing this poignant tale can be seen at the Gadsden site. A companion plaque at Fort San Marcos de Apalache repeats the tale of Florida's Pocahontas, Milly.

A steamboat, the *Irvington,* burned and sank in the river four miles upstream from the fort site in 1838. The rusting boilers and some of the works thought to be from this ship were dredged from the river and can still be seen at the site. During the Civil War, Confederate troops briefly occupied the fort.

The State of Florida conducted archaeological work and then turned the site over to the U.S. Forest Service for administration in 1978.

6

Fort San Marcos de Apalache

Location: 148 Old Fort Road, St. Marks Florida, about 20 miles south of Tallahassee.
Driving Directions: From Tallahassee, go about 20 miles due south on SR 363. In the town of St. Marks, turn right on Old Fort Road and watch for signs indicating a left turn into the fort site grounds.
Hours of Operation: 9 a.m. to 5 p.m., Thursday to Monday. Closed Tuesday and Wednesday. Also closed on Thanksgiving, Christmas, and New Year's Day.
Fees: No admission charge to enter the park; the museum fee is $2 per person for those who wish to view the video.
Phone: (850) 925-6216

Unique Facts

Several forts were built at the junction of two rivers, the Wakulla and the St. Marks, to guard passage to the interior; the Spanish built a fort here beginning in 1679 as one of the earliest fortified places in West Florida; the fort later saw a major confrontation between the United States and Britain after the War of 1812. Still later, the fort was the site of a U.S. Marine Hospital.

This Spanish cannon is on display at the entrance to the visitor center. (Loretta Carlisle photo.)

Things to See

The museum displays in the visitor center give a detailed history of the site. The museum/visitor center is built on the site of the Marine Hospital built in the 1850s, using stones from earlier fortifications for the foundation that can be readily viewed under the concrete walls of the newer structure. A marked trail through the park takes the visitor to foundations and sites of the early forts. Before taking the walk, visitors should pick up the brief brochure from the visitor center that identifies the sites.

Things to See Nearby

Fort Gadsden is about two hours to the west via US 319; the lighthouse in the town of St. Marks is a notable local landmark; the site of the Battle of Natural Bridge is about 10 miles due north on Old Plank Road out of St. Marks. Mission San Luis, in Tallahassee, gives details of the early settlement and fortification of the area by the Spanish.

At the San Marcos de Apalache State Historic Site, the ruins of the Spanish fort walls can be traced through the lush vegetation. Numbered stations provide an informative guide. (Loretta Carlisle photo.)

History

In 1528, the Spanish explorer Pánfilo de Narváez passed this way with a force of three hundred men. Narváez stopped at the junction of the Wakulla and St. Marks Rivers, where his troops built and launched the first ships made by Europeans in the New World. A few years later, in 1539, the explorer Hernando de Soto more or less followed the Narváez route from Tampa through central and northwestern Florida. He marked the spot with flags and banners to identify the river's entrance, about where the modern lighthouse is located.

About 1679, the Spanish began construction on the first fort built at the point, covering logs with a lime coating so they would appear to be made of stone. The fort lasted only a short time before pirates burned it. In 1718, Spanish Capt. Jose Primo de Ribera led a group that built the second wooden fort at the site. The Spanish followed with some beginnings on the first stone fort in 1739. In 1758, a hurricane flooded the fort, drowning

This idealized depiction of de Soto's first arrival in Florida was published in *Ballou's Pictorial* in 1855. The expedition did, in fact, include more than six hundred men, women, and servants so the numbers shown here are no exaggeration. (Courtesy of the Library of Congress.)

some forty men. The Spanish had not even half-built the fort when they ceded Florida to Britain at the end of the Seven Years' War in 1763. After the American Revolution, in 1787, Spain took back control of the fort. However, the province of West Florida remained a remote part of the Spanish Empire, subject to pirate raids, restive Creek and Seminole Native Americans who resented the incursion of white settlers, and fugitive slaves fleeing from slavery in Georgia. The small garrison of Spanish troops at San Marcos made no effort to patrol the long, unmarked border between Spanish West Florida and the United States. The unsettled conditions left the region open to adventurers.

In 1800, an American Loyalist by the name of William Augustus Bowles attempted to set up an independent state made up of Creek Indians, and his forces laid siege to Fort San Marcos de Apalache. Bowles appointed himself "Director General and Commander-In-Chief of the Muskogee Nation" and mounted an armed effort to take on both Spain and the United States in establishing his separate country with the help of fugitive slaves, white Bahamian pirates and adventurers, Spanish deserters, and Seminole and Creek Indians. The Spanish arrived with a fleet of nine ships and drove Bowles off. The Spanish eventually captured Bowles and imprisoned him in Morro Castle in Cuba, where he died in 1805.

However, the region remained lawless. Gen. Andrew Jackson, operating out of Georgia, ordered U.S. forces against the British-built fort that had been taken over by fugitive slaves a few miles west, at what is now Fort Gadsden. A combined force of U.S. Army and Navy ships attacked the "Negro Fort," and a lucky shot blew up the fort and most of its three hundred defenders. Two

Andrew Jackson led U.S. troops into Spanish Florida and arrested and executed British subjects engaged in trading guns and other goods to Seminoles and African American refugees from slavery. (Courtesy of the Library of Congress.)

years later, in 1817–18, Jackson personally invaded West Florida again, and seized San Marcos de Apalache. Gen. Edmund Gaines, who would have led the attack, could not do so because at the time he was fighting near Fernandina (on Amelia Island, north of present-day Jacksonville) to suppress a budding pirate state there.

In a notorious episode that won him criticism but not formal censure in Congress and widespread approval among the American public, Jackson captured two British citizens, Robert Ambrister and Alexander Arbuthnot. Arbuthnot traded out of the Bahamas with the local Native Americans, most probably supplying them with guns. Jackson suspected Robert Ambrister, a former British marine and self-appointed "Indian agent," of complicity in gunrunning. Jackson accused them both of trading arms to the local Seminoles and Creeks as well as to the fugitive slaves seeking sanctuary among them. Although a local U.S. military tribunal found both guilty and sentenced them to death, the court then remitted the punishment to public lashing and a year in prison. Jackson overrode the decision and had both men executed. A firing squad shot Ambrister, as befitting an officer, and Jackson ordered Arbuthnot hanged from the yardarm of his own trading ship, the *Chance*. The "Ambrister and Arbuthnot Affair" created a diplomatic crisis with Britain, and Jackson withdrew his forces from San Marcos and began his next move against Pensacola. The fort, known to the British as Fort St. Marks, returned to Spanish jurisdiction.

In 1821, when Spain ceded Florida to the United States under the Adams-Onis Treaty, U.S. troops were dispatched to take over the fort. But in 1824, the U.S. Army pulled out and turned the fort over to the Territory of Florida. In 1841, the U.S. Supreme Court ruled that the fort remained a military reserve, under the jurisdiction of the U.S. government. Congress did not admit Florida into Union until 1845, after the Second Seminole War. In the practice at the time, Congress admitted two states at a time, one slave and one free, with Iowa as a free state matching Florida as a slave state, to maintain the balance in Congress. In the mid-1850s, the government began building a marine hospital on the

At the ruins of Fort San Marcos de Apalache (Fort St. Marks, to the British), the visitor can see that the bastions commanded a clear line of shot for guarding passage up the Wakulla River. (Loretta Carlisle photo.)

site of San Marcos de Apalache, using the stones from the Spanish fort as part of the foundation. The marine hospital treated victims of yellow fever, the result of several epidemics through the 1850s.

In the first years of the Civil War, the Confederates took over the fort, renaming it Fort Ward. As part of the Union blockade, a squadron of U.S. ships blocked the mouth of the St. Marks River. A land battle known as the Battle of Natural Bridge, fought nearby on March 5, 1865, stopped Union troops marching overland with naval support in an attempt to reach the fort. The fight at Natural Bridge kept Tallahassee as the only southern capital east of the Mississippi not conquered by Union forces during the Civil War.

On November 13, 1966, after archaeological work, the Fort San Marcos de Apalache was designated a National Historic Landmark and added to the U.S. National Register of Historic Places. The Florida State Park system administers San Marcos de Apalache.

7

Mission San Luis

Location: In Tallahassee at 2100 West Tennessee Street, about one mile west of the State Capitol.
Driving Directions: *From west on I-10*, take exit 196, and head south on SR 263 (Capital Circle NW) to West Tennessee Street; turn left and proceed about 3 miles to entrance to Mission San Luis. *From east on I-10*, take exit 199; bear south on North Monroe Street about 4 miles; turn right on Tennessee Street and proceed about 2.5 miles. San Luis Mission is on the right, just after the East Towne Shopping Center.
Hours of Operation: 10 a.m. to 4 p.m., Tuesday through Sunday. Closed Monday.
Fees: Adults, $5; seniors (65 and over), $3; children (6–17), $2; active-duty military, free with ID.
Phone: (850) 245-6406

Unique Facts

The fort here is a reproduction and the only fort in Florida associated with a Catholic mission from the Spanish colonial period. The site served as a mission settlement for the Apalachee people, and as the capital of West Florida under Spanish rule from 1656 to 1704. The base of a limestone baptismal font found at the site is unique, the only remains of a baptismal font ever located at a mission in Spanish Florida.

The entrance to the exhibit hall and offices at Mission San Luis replicates Spanish Mission–style architecture. (Loretta Carlisle photo.)

Things to See

The plaza where the Apalachee people played traditional ball games; reconstruction-replicas of the Apalachee council house; the home of the Spanish deputy governor; fort grounds and interior of the fort; church built under the supervision of Franciscan missionaries, and the friary or residence of the missionaries. The council house is quite unique, a thatched conical structure some 119 feet in diameter with a large central hole at the top. The modern replica faithfully follows most of the original layout, with an outer and inner ring of benches, and a central hearth. In colonial times, tenders kept a fire burning in the center day and night. Visitors to the settlement, both Native American and Spanish, would be housed on the outer ring of benches, which were divided by partitions into small compartments, or "cabins." The guests kept smudge pots burning, often directly under the benches, with corn husks as fuel, to keep away mosquitoes and other insects.

Costumed interpreters are usually present to explain the details of the council house, the church, and other structures. At

In the late seventeenth century, visitors to the mission would be assigned a compartment on the benches lining the exterior wall of the council house. (Loretta Carlisle photo.)

the fort itself, the interpreters explain daily life, military details, and fort construction specifics, and provide well-informed answers to questions from visitors.

Fort San Luis, at the north end of the mission grounds, is a replica of the original fort, with a surrounding stockade supported by banked earthen ramparts. The fort consists of a central structure or citadel that served as a barracks for the Spanish soldiers, protected by the strong outer wall of earth and timber. A tour of the citadel gives a glimpse of the soldiers' life during the Spanish mission era. Displays include weapons, utensils, tools, and a powder magazine. Soldiers and Apalachee allies displayed a banner with an image of the Our Lady of the Rosary, carried on expeditions as a battle standard.

Unique features of the fort include gun ports placed high on the walls, and a small trench outside the walls of the fort, originally planted with cactus (as there was insufficient water to maintain a moat). The present palisade around the fort grounds is actually constructed of concrete, formed in molds to represent sharpened logs, a practical solution that looks exactly like the original but does not require periodic replacement of rotted wooden palisade

Costumed interpreters provide detailed explanations for visitors to the fort's interior. (Loretta Carlisle photo.)

posts. The wall of the fort itself was made of pine planking, reinforced on the inside with a type of plaster known as "wattle-and-daub." The original pine planking was 3 inches thick; however, the fort construction would not have withstood bombardment by cannon, one of the reasons the defenders abandoned the fort in 1704.

The corners of the palisade enclosure have projecting bastions, allowing muskets or small cannon placed inside the bastion to

The gate through the palisade welcomes visitors to the reconstructed fort grounds. (Loretta Carlisle photo.)

These corner bastions mounted large muskets or small cannons to protect the walls against attack. (Loretta Carlisle photo.)

have fields of fire along the outside of the palisade in case of attack.

Things to See Nearby

About 21 miles to the south is Fort San Marcos de Apalache (Fort St. Marks), occupied by the Spanish in the same era; Fort Gadsden is about 70 miles to the west.

History

Mission San Luis and its fort tell the story of the Apalachee Indian people who lived in West Florida prior to and after the arrival of the Spanish in the sixteenth century and of the Spanish governance of the area through the seventeenth century. Archaeologists and historians have uncovered the history of the settlement, and the modern reconstruction of structures and the layout of the fort reflect extensive research into the period of Spanish–Indian contact prior to 1704. The replica structures are built a few feet offset from the original location so that further archaeological work can be done.

The site at San Luis (near the center of Tallahassee) represented the central community of the Apalachee people who occupied a territory between the Ochlocknee and the Lucille Rivers in western Florida and southern Georgia prior to Spanish contact. Shortly after the foundation of St. Augustine in 1565, the Spanish established numerous missions in northern Florida. They built a mission at Apalachee 1633, although some Apalachee had asked for friars to be sent to the region much earlier.

That mission and fort evolved to become a thriving municipality. By 1656, the settlement represented the Spanish administrative capital of West Florida. A king's highway, or *camino real*, connected San Luis to St. Augustine, linking San Luis with Fort San Marcos de Apalache (Fort St. Marks) and with missions among the Apalachee and Timucua peoples scattered across northern Florida. Research has indicated that the Spanish religious and civil administration of the region tended to allow local control by Native Americans of their community affairs, while Catholic mission friars allowed a degree of blending of Native American religious practices with the Catholicism in such details as burial practices. The Apalachee were willing converts to Catholicism, and followed Catholic practices of baptism, marriage, and attendance at Mass. The sites of sixteen of the missions from the era have been identified.

Behind the cannons on display on the fort grounds are the firing ports in the palisade wall. (Loretta Carlisle photo.)

After the establishment of South Carolina by English settlers from Barbados in 1670 and the introduction there of plantation slavery with African American slaves, pressures built on the Spanish settlements of North Florida. Florida became a battleground in the wars for empire, including Queen Anne's War (1702–13), with a British invasion of Florida in 1702. Settlers, Apalachee, and refugees from other tribes at San Luis, fearing the British attack and acting on orders from the Spanish governor, burned the mission, council house, and fort to the ground in July 1704. They then fled prior to the arrival of the invaders. The evacuating caravan left with oxcarts and on foot, and included some eight hundred men, women, and children. The fears were proven to be well grounded, as more than eight thousand people in northern Florida were removed and enslaved by the English invaders under Governor James Moore of South Carolina.

In North America, the French and English fought much of Queen Anne's War in what is now Massachusetts, Maine, and Newfoundland. As a result of the war, France ceded control of Acadia, Newfoundland, Hudson Bay (in what is now Canada), and the island of St. Kitts to Britain. However, Spain retained control of Florida.

Although the war did not lead to significant territorial boundary changes in the South, it did have a disastrous effect in Florida. There, the British invasion nearly wiped out the Indian population, and destroyed the Spanish mission network across northern Florida. Although the Apalachee from San Luis scattered, many of them settled in French-controlled Mobile, and later, in 1763, a group of some eighty surviving Apalachee moved on to Rapides Parish in Louisiana. Recent research has demonstrated that descendents of those people still reside in Louisiana, many in Natchitoches Parish immediately to the northwest of Rapides Parish. Many have returned to visit the site of their ancestral home at the invitation of the State of Florida.

The Bureau of Archaeological Research of the Division of Historical Resources, Florida Department of State, administers the mission and its fort.

2 Northeast Florida

8

Camp Blanding

Location: 9 miles east of Starke.
Driving Directions: *From the north*, drive south on US 301 through Lawtey to Starke. *From Gainesville and Waldo*, drive north on 301 to Starke. When driving on this stretch of US 301, scrupulously obey the speed limits, which change every few miles; Lawtey and Waldo are well-known speed traps, with billboards warning to that effect. At Starke, turn east on SR 16 and travel about 9 miles to the Camp Blanding Main Gate/Museum entrance; turn right and park in one of the designated areas.
Hours of Operation: Noon to 4 p.m. daily. Closed Easter, Thanksgiving, Christmas, and New Year's Day.
Fees: No admission charge; donations accepted.
Phone: (904) 682-3196

Unique Facts

During World War II, Camp Blanding held so many troops that only Tampa, Miami, and Jacksonville exceeded it in population, making Camp Blanding the fourth-largest "city" in Florida. At its largest extent, 170,000 acres, Camp Blanding became the second-largest training facility in the United States. The camp is built around Lake Kingsley, a unique lake in that it is perfectly round, about 2.5 miles in diameter. Its round shape is thought by some to be the result of a prehistoric meteor impact; it is fed by freshwater springs so that it never runs dry.

The museum marks the entrance to Camp Blanding outside the gate, restricting admission to the military base. (Loretta Carlisle photo.)

Things to See

The base is still used as a National Guard facility and for training of other military and law-enforcement units, so visiting is limited to the museum. Only those on official business or with military IDs can enter the base itself. The museum houses a collection of weapons (U.S. and foreign) and is located in a refurbished World War II building that once served as a guest house for families visiting the base; today only the first floor is open to visitors, while the second floor is used for storage of further collections. The exhibits tell the story of Camp Blanding, the units that trained there and some of their overseas assignments, and the nearby area of Florida during World War II. On the grounds are displays of World War II–era military vehicles and weapons, as well as a Douglas C-47 SkyTrain aircraft similar to those that saw service in Sicily, Burma, and France during World War II. Adjacent to the museum is the Florida Regimental Memorial, dominated by the statue of a soldier. The memorial shows the areas of war service by Florida National Guard units and a roster of Florida Guardsmen who lost their lives in service.

The Memorial Park is a large military memorabilia exhibition area containing monuments honoring nine Army Infantry Divisions and the 508th Parachute Infantry Regiment, all of whom trained at Camp Blanding. The "Borne Monument," a French historical highway marker, came from Liberty Road in Normandy, and the French presented it to the Camp Blanding Museum, dedicated on VE Day, May 8, 1998. This marker came from the first town in France liberated by the Thirtieth Infantry Division.

Things to See Nearby

Starke is rather isolated from other forts and military sites of interest; it is 55 miles due west of St. Augustine on SR 16, a trip of about an hour and twenty minutes. However, the Military Museum of North Florida is maintained at Green Cove Springs, about 20 miles east of Camp Blanding, housing displays of military artifacts from the colonial period to the present, open 10 a.m. to 3 p.m., Tuesday through Saturday. The private museum is located at 901 Bunker Avenue, just south of SR 16.

Flags at the Memorial flew at half-mast in January 2011, in response to the shooting of Arizona congresswoman Gabrielle Giffords and the deaths of six others. (Loretta Carlisle photo.)

History

Camp Blanding had its origins in 1939, when the conversion of an Air National Guard base in Jacksonville into a Naval Air Station led to the search for a new location for an Air National Guard base. The National Guard chose isolated flat land near Starke, originally consisting of 28,200 acres, and named it after Gen. Albert H. Blanding, who had served in the U.S. Army from 1894 to 1940, ending his career commanding the Thirty-first Division.

During World War II, Camp Blanding rapidly expanded, and became an advanced training base for troops prior to their dispatch overseas. Rapid construction methods evolved, allowing the cutting of lumber, framing, and complete building of a standard mess hall in less than an hour. Some 125 miles of road were laid. As troops practiced close-order drill, they had to be marched on the paved roads because of the ankle-deep sand.

A boomtown housing bars, brothels, and shops sprang up along SR 16 near the entrance to Camp Blanding, with a scattering of trailers and temporary buildings built from scrap lumber. At the time, the small country town of Starke was little more than a spot on the road with no facilities for guests or travelers.

The first unit trained at Camp Blanding, the Thirty-first Infantry Division, represented National Guard troops called up from Louisiana, Mississippi, Alabama, and Florida, nicknamed the "Dixie Darlings." Soon, the Forty-third Infantry Division followed, drawn from the New England states of Connecticut, Rhode Island, Vermont, and Maine. The rivalry between the Dixie and Yankee troops became intense, with an imaginary dividing "Mason-Dixie" line bisecting the base more or less at the parade grounds.

These two divisions that trained at the base prior to the attack on Pearl Harbor were the first divisions taking advanced infantry training at Camp Blanding during the war. The Thirty-first and Forty-third Divisions were both shipped to the Pacific Theater and did not return to the United States until the end of the war. Other divisions that trained at Camp Blanding, and that saw service in the European Theater, were the Thirty-sixth

Colloquially known as a "duck," this six-wheeled vehicle was used in amphibious attacks on beaches. (Loretta Carlisle photo.)

National Guard Division from Texas, the Regular Army First Division, the Seventy-ninth Reserve Division, the Twenty-ninth National Guard Division (drawn from mid-Atlantic States), and the Thirtieth National Guard Division from North Carolina, South Carolina, Tennessee, and Georgia. The Twentieth Engineer Combat Regiment trained there in early 1942. In addition, two engineer regiments, both made up of African American troops, trained at Camp Blanding—the Forty-fifth and Ninety-seventh Engineer General Service Regiments. They went on to crucial construction jobs such as the Alcan Highway (from Washington State to Alaska), roadwork in North Africa and the Lido Road in Burma, and other assignments. Units smaller than division-size also trained at Camp Blanding, including the 508th Parachute Infantry, the 102nd, 91st, 124th, and 156th Infantry Regiments, the 6th Cavalry Regiment, the 631st, 643rd, and 774th Tank Destroyer Battalions, the 74th Field Artillery Brigade, and the 141st, 166th, 17th, 35th, and 179th Field Artillery Regiments. Five Field Artillery Battalions also trained there: the 932nd, 934th, 935th, 938th, and 939th.

Army historians estimate that some eight hundred thousand soldiers received training at Camp Blanding during the war.

Toward the end of the war, Camp Blanding became a POW camp for captured German prisoners, with some one thousand

Vehicles on display outside the museum include this World War II–vintage ambulance. (Loretta Carlisle photo.)

prisoners housed at Blanding and an additional two thousand housed at other camps under Camp Blanding's administration. At the end of the war, with demobilization and the reduction of bases, some 30,000 acres of the camp were returned to the State of Florida.

Today the Camp Blanding Joint Training Center is the primary training base for the Florida National Guard and Florida Air National Guard. The site is now about 73,000 acres, including Kingsley Lake. Camp Blanding also is the site for a variety of other Reserve, Army National Guard, Air National Guard, and some Active Component training for the U.S. armed forces including the headquarters and support companies of the 3–20th Special Forces Group, the 211th Infantry Regiment, and the 2–111th Airfield Operations Battalion (AOB) Aviation Regiment.

Camp Blanding is also the base for several ground-based units of the Florida Air National Guard, including the 202nd Red Horse Squadron, 159th Weather Flight, Weather Readiness Training Center (WRTC), and the joint Army/Air Force 44th Civil Support Team. The base is also a training center for a variety of counterdrug units and law enforcement agencies. The barracks and housing facilities can now house up to three thousand personnel, in four Battalion Areas, each with its own mess hall, barracks, supply buildings, and headquarters building.

Training Areas on the base include three Major Maneuver Areas with a total of 55,000 acres including planted pine plantations, swamps, oak hammocks, and desert terrain. There is also a Military Operations in Urban Terrain (MOUT) Collective Training Facility that is made up of sixteen buildings and other facilities. The base also hosts a bombing and strafing target area for military aircraft, situated at the southern end of the camp. None of these facilities is open for visits by tourists.

The exhibits in the museum building give an excellent depiction of life at the base during World War II, with photos and structural displays. Soldiers were housed in tents and "hutments" or wood-framed and floored structures with canvas roofs, heated by small wood stoves, and a mock-up of the interior of a hutment in the museum shows conditions of wartime living. Other displays with mannequins show uniforms, equipment, weaponry, and aspects of daily life of both U.S. troops and enemy troops during World War II.

Uniformed mannequins appear in several of the displays inside the Camp Blanding Museum, like this re-creation of a manned communications center. (Loretta Carlisle photo.)

9

Fort Clinch

Location: On the north end of Amelia Island, facing the entrance of St. Marys River into Cumberland Sound from the Atlantic Ocean. Address: 2601 Atlantic Avenue, Fernandina Beach.
Driving Directions: From downtown Fernandina Beach, follow SR 200 (Atlantic Avenue, Florida A1A) east toward the ocean. The well-marked entrance to the park is on the left at Fort Clinch Road.
Hours of Operation: 8 a.m. until sundown, 365 days per year.
Fees: $6 per car ($4 single-occupant car).
Phone: (904) 277-7274

Special Events

Summer candlelight tours from May to September (except Saturdays during First Weekend Garrisons). The first Saturday of every month, groups of costumed interpreters offer a view of garrison life from the Civil War period. Evening candlelight tours of Fort Clinch are led by a costumed Union soldier interpreter through the historic fort. The narration includes tales of a soldier's life in 1864. Reservations are required, and the fees for the tour are $3 per person in addition to the park entrance fee. Tour times vary with sundown, and reservations should be confirmed by phone.

Unique Facts

Fort Clinch never saw action in any military battles, although Confederate troops and Union troops occupied the fort during

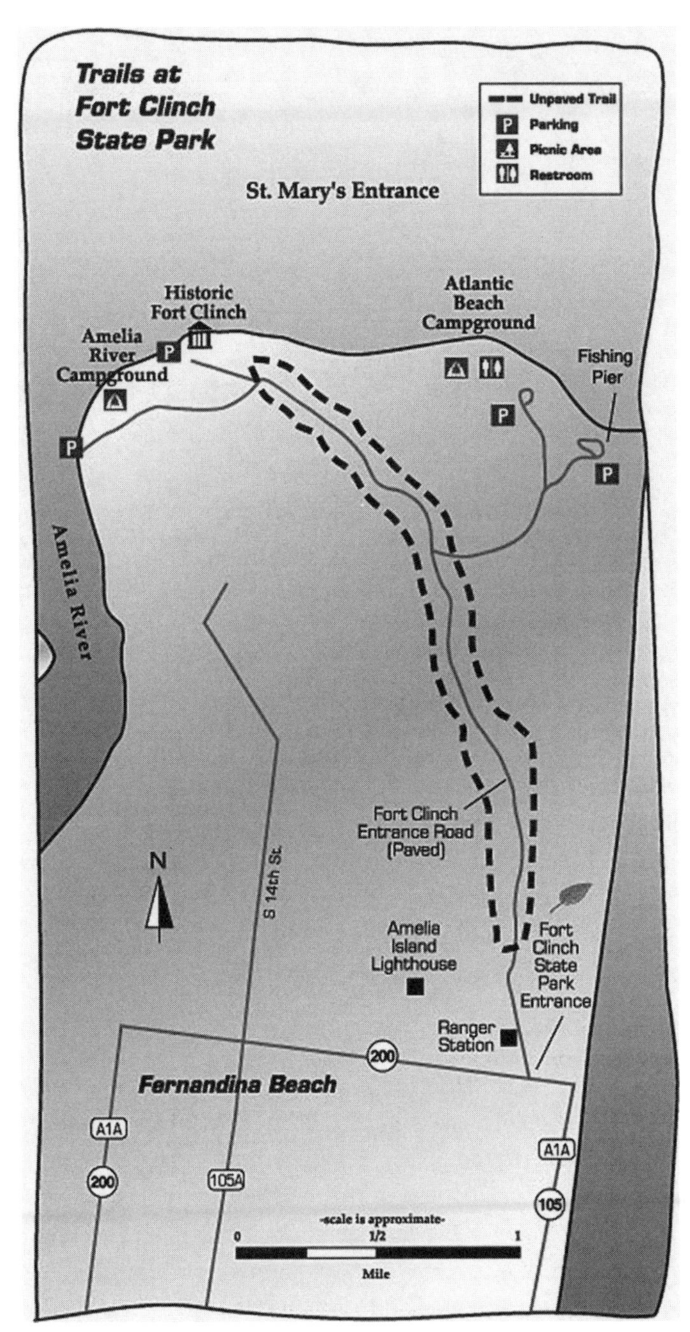

Map of Fort Clinch State Park, showing the fort's location inside the larger park. (Loretta Carlisle photo of Florida State Park map.)

Fort Clinch has an extensive parade ground surrounded by high masonry walls. (Loretta Carlisle photo.)

the American Civil War. The Army never actually completed construction on the fort, and brought the work there to a halt two years after the end of the Civil War. On March 2, 1862, the U.S gunboat *Ottawa* fired on a Confederate steam train that departed from Fernandina with the evacuating Confederate troops aboard, the first recorded time in history that a warship fired on a moving train. The movie *Sunshine State* featured the fort, in which one of the characters was a reenactor.

Things to See

The fort is an excellent example of a Third System Fortification (those built in the period 1812–68 of masonry and earth). There are some artifacts on display, and the rooms include a prison/guardhouse, a bakery, a blacksmith shop, officers' and enlisted men's barrack quarters, a kitchen and laundry, and latrines. Access to the outer curtain wall and bastions is open, although care should be taken on steep stairs and on the walls. Volunteer costumed interpreters provide information.

Things to See Nearby

The historic town of Fernandina, with shops and restaurants, is a pleasant walking venue. For a period in the nineteenth century, Fernandina became a leading resort in Florida for visitors from the North, especially in the early Gilded Age decades of the 1870s and 1880s, before St. Augustine became the primary Florida attraction. Elegant Victorian homes from that era make the city somewhat unique in Florida. The fort's surrounding park has a 6-mile trail for hikers or bicyclists, with self-guided nature walks. A full-facility campground and a youth camping area provide for overnight stays. Swimming and beachcombing are favorite activities along the shoreline. For military history tourists, it is less than an hour's drive from Fort Clinch to Fort Caroline, east of Jacksonville; those especially interested in Civil War history should take note of the fort's strategic location near Fernandina, the eastern terminus of the Florida Railroad, which crossed Florida from coast to coast, with its western terminus at Cedar Key on the Gulf. The closure of Fernandina to international shipping early in 1862 advanced the Union's so-called "Anaconda" strategy of closing off seaports and blockading the southern coast during the Civil War.

At Fort Clinch, costumed interpreters play the roles of Union troops at the fort in the 1860s; this sergeant is sewing on his stripes. (Loretta Carlisle photo.)

History

By early in the nineteenth century, Amelia Island and Fernandina had gained a reputation for harboring pirates and smugglers. Hundreds of slaves were smuggled into Georgia and the United States after the 1808 banning of the international slave trade. In fact, in 1817, a Scots adventurer named Gregor MacGregor, with a force of fifty-five musketeers, captured the Spanish Fort San Carlos and raised a flag with a green cross on behalf of Buenos Aires, Mexico, New Grenada, and Venezuela. After Spanish forces drove him off, the "pirate" Luis Aury sailed into Fernandina, took over in the name of the Republic of Mexico (then still governed by Spain), and declared himself ruler. He had previously ruled over Galveston, Texas, in the name of independent Mexico, but turned that command over to Jean and Pierre Lafitte. Over the next few months, the lawless outpost on Amelia Island under Aury saw smugglers of luxury goods, pirates, and outlaws operating freely there. Aury developed his own flag with a sword crossed with an olive branch. The U.S. Navy chased out Aury by 1818. Records are unclear as to whether he died in Old Providence Island off Nicaragua (which he also briefly governed), or whether he survived another two decades.

The U.S. government purchased the land for the construction of Fort Clinch in 1842, choosing the spot on the northern end of Amelia Island to protect the entrance to Cumberland Sound and the St. Marys River, which forms the border between Florida and Georgia in this area. The fort would guard the mouth of the river, protect coastal and inland shipping, and serve as a defense of the deepwater seaport of Fernandina. Construction began in 1847. The government named the fort, like many in Florida, after an officer who had commanded in Florida's Seminole Wars, in this case, Gen. Duncan Lamont Clinch. Clinch had led the American forces at the destruction of "the Negro Fort," or Fort Gadsden.

Work on the brick fort moved slowly. By 1860–61, when the election of Abraham Lincoln spurred the secession of several states of the South, only two bastions and about a third of the outer brick wall had been completed. Builders finished the

While transporting troops and supplies, the Union steamers *Maple Leaf* and *Genl. Hunter* were sunk by mines (then called "torpedoes") in the St. Johns River near Fort Clinch. The wreck of the *Maple Leaf* has been recently identified at the river bottom. (An 1864 drawing by Alfred R. Waud. Courtesy of the Library of Congress.)

guardhouse/prison, and surrounded the fort with outer ramparts, but were still working on other rooms. They had not placed any cannons at the fort. Early in 1861, as Florida prepared for secession, Florida militia quietly occupied the uncompleted fort. The militia troops hauled in some guns, and set up batteries in the port of Fernandina and on various locations on Amelia and Cumberland Islands. By December 1861, Confederate militias and army troops stationed at the fort numbered 1,524. However, they fought no battles at or near the fort, and on March 2, 1862, Confederates evacuated the fort, just as Union gunboats arrived.

The Civil War historian Lewis Zerfas has uncovered the story. Pro-Union residents of Fernandina sent word to Lt. Cmdr. T. H. Stevens, captain of the gunboat *Ottawa*, that Confederate troops had boarded a train to evacuate. The gunboat pulled within range of the train, and troops aboard the train jeered at the naval vessel, some firing their muskets and rifles at the ship. The *Ottawa* trailed the departing troop train for two or three miles in the shallow river system, firing the 11-inch pivot Dahlgren aboard, trying to disable the two steam engines pulling the train. One shell killed two men, M. Savage and John M. Thompson, on a flatcar hauled by the train. Sources do not reveal the background of these two men, who did not appear on the Confederate rosters for the fort.

David Levy Yulee, a former U.S. senator from Florida (the first U.S. senator of Jewish descent), and the founder and chief financier of the Florida Railroad, made his escape from Union capture aboard the train. A fragment from one of the shells from the *Ottawa* fatally wounded the man sitting next to Yulee. Yulee remained committed to the Confederate cause throughout the war. The town of Yulee, Florida, named after the senator, is about 9 miles west of the community of Fernandina Beach.

While the ship fired on the train, the conductor cut loose some of the rear cars, and the engineer put on extra steam. Finally, after two hours, the train successfully crossed the bridge to the mainland. The *Ottawa* could follow no farther. Later, Confederates returned and burned the railroad bridge, cutting Fernandina off from land transport to the interior of Florida.

Fort Clinch became the first Confederate fortress in Florida restored to Federal control by this action of the *Ottawa,* backed up by twenty-seven other gunboats in the Union flotilla. Troops from the First New York Volunteer Engineers moved into the fort and began work on completing the construction. The kitchen, mess hall, barracks rooms, magazines, and workshops made the fort slightly more comfortable for the troops.

Confederate regiments that had served either at Fort Clinch or in defense of the town of Fernandina included the Third, Fourth, and Tenth Florida Infantry; the Twenty-fourth Mississippi Infantry; the Second Florida Cavalry; the Palatka Guard; units of the Florida Militia; and an unattached artillery battery. Union regiments included the Sixth and Seventh Connecticut Infantry; the First New York Engineers; the Ninth and Eleventh Maine Infantry; the Fourth and Seventh New Hampshire Infantry; the Ninety-seventh Pennsylvania Infantry; the 157th New York Infantry, and the Seventh United States Infantry. African American Union forces included the First South Carolina Infantry, and

Within the walls of Fort Clinch are rooms devoted to barracks, workshops, mess halls, and the brig. (Loretta Carlisle photo.)

the First, Third, Twenty-first, and Thirty-fourth United States Colored Troops. Meanwhile, the Union Navy blockaded the St. Johns River with seagoing vessels and commandeered local steamers.

When Union forces bombarded Fort Pulaski, Georgia, on April 10, 1862, that shelling demonstrated that the new naval ordnance, fired from rifled cannon, could destroy brick walls. With this battle, military engineers recognized that the "Third System" had become obsolete. Intermittent efforts continued to finish construction on Fort Clinch, but all work halted in 1867, and the fort went on the inactive list.

The fort remained inactive for three decades after 1869, with the departure of the last U.S. troops under Reconstruction in that year. However, when the Spanish-American War began in 1898, the War Department reactivated the fort, as Americans feared Spanish forces would attack the U.S. mainland. Battery A of the Sixth U.S. Artillery arrived at the dilapidated and long-abandoned fort. The troops repaired damage and built a mount for an 8-inch breech-loading artillery piece. The gun mount can be seen on the northeast parapet of the fort, but engineers never mounted the gun. The troops evacuated after the end of the brief war, in September 1898.

During World War I, the War Department once again activated the fort. The Coast Guard, working with the Army and Navy, set up a communications and surveillance system along the coast, using the fort as a base. The Coast Guard established a horse-mounted beach patrol that scouted the beaches for possible landings by enemy spies and saboteurs.

The U.S. government sold the land and fort to private interests in 1926, and then in 1935, the State of Florida bought the fort and the surrounding land for outdoor recreation purposes. During the 1930s, the federal Civilian Conservation Corps (CCC) assisted in developing the trails and facilities in Fort Clinch State Park.

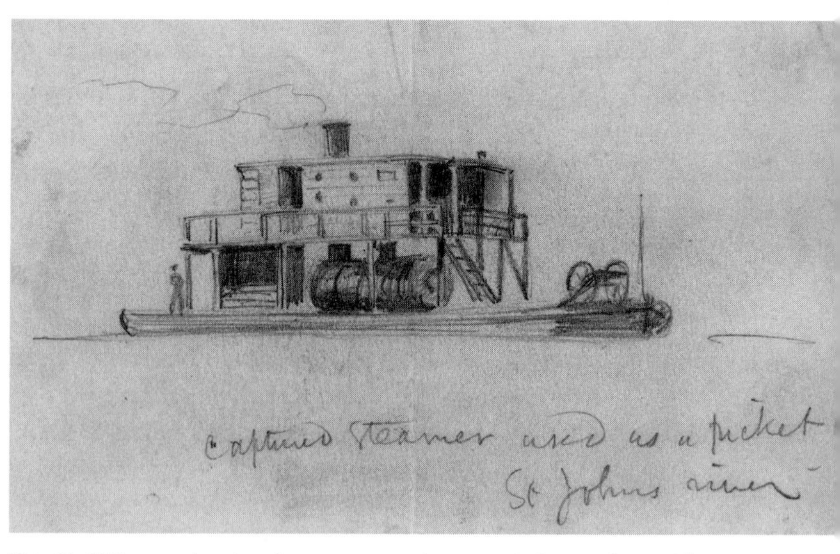

This Civil War–era drawing shows a captured steamer being used as a picket boat by Union forces on the St. Johns River, not far from Fort Clinch. (Drawing by Alfred R. Waud, ca. 1860–65. Courtesy of the Library of Congress.)

On the top of the outer wall at Fort Clinch, these 10-inch Rodman guns look over the broad reach of the Atlantic toward barrier islands off the Georgia shore. (Loretta Carlisle photo.)

10

Fort Caroline

Location: 13 miles east of Jacksonville.
Directions: Follow Arlington Expressway (SR 115, Alternative US 1/US 90) east to Monument Road, then east on Fort Caroline Road. Entrance is on the left. *From the north*, exit from I-95 to SR 9A; cross the St. Johns River, exit on Monument Road, east; then go east on Fort Caroline Road to fort entrance on left.
Hours of Operation: 9 a.m. to 5 p.m. daily. Closed Christmas, Thanksgiving, and New Year's Day.
Fees: No admission charge. The park is a National Memorial operated by the National Park Service.
Phone: (904) 641-7155
Note: Mosquito repellent is advised for those hiking the extensive Spanish Road Trail into the Theodore Roosevelt Area to the east of the memorial. The Preserve includes 46,000 acres, including the Kingsley Plantation and lands on both sides of the St. Johns River, as well as the Fort Caroline National Memorial.

Unique Facts

The first European settlement in what is now the continental United States came at Fort Caroline, preceding St. Augustine, Florida (by one year), and Jamestown, Virginia, and Santa Fe, New Mexico (both by forty-three years). However, since settlers and troops abandoned the fort, it is not the oldest continuous European settlement in the continental United States; St. Augustine has that distinction. (Native Americans recaptured Santa

This 1591 engraving of the building of Fort Caroline captures the outline of the fort but errs in showing it located on a separate island of its own. (Theodor de Bry, after a watercolor by Jacques Le Moyne. Courtesy of the Library of Congress.)

Fort Caroline gate. The gate, like the rest of the fort, is built at one-third scale of the original. (Loretta Carlisle photo.)

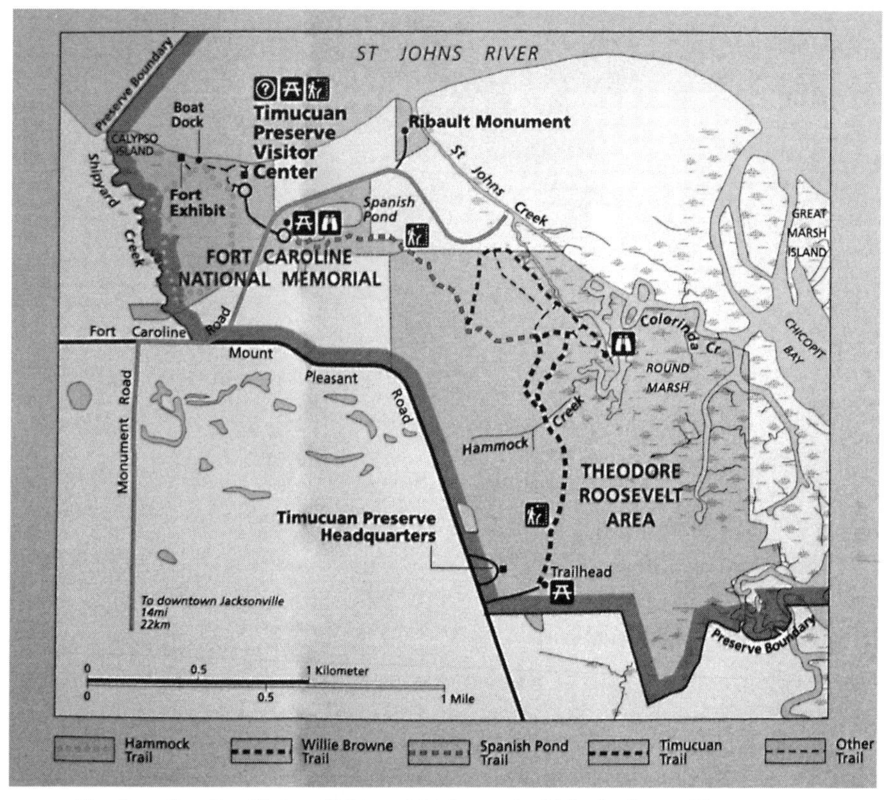

The Fort Caroline National Memorial is located within the larger Timucuan Ecological and Historical Preserve, maintained by the National Park Service. (Loretta Carlisle Photo of National Park Service map.)

Fe, New Mexico, in the period 1680–92, during the time of the "Pueblo Revolt," so people of European ancestry have continuously occupied that city only since 1692.)

Things to See

The visitor center has displays explaining the natural and human history of the site, with excellent materials on the Timucua Native Americans.

The fort itself is at the edge of the St. Johns River, a few hundred yards by easy and clearly marked trail to the left of the center and the parking lot. On the way to the fort, there is a small

This 1590 Theodor de Bry engraving shows the Timucua method of cooking or smoking fish. (After a watercolor by John White. Courtesy of the Library of Congress.)

As a protection against accidental fire, baking was done outside the fort in just such an oven. (Loretta Carlisle photo.)

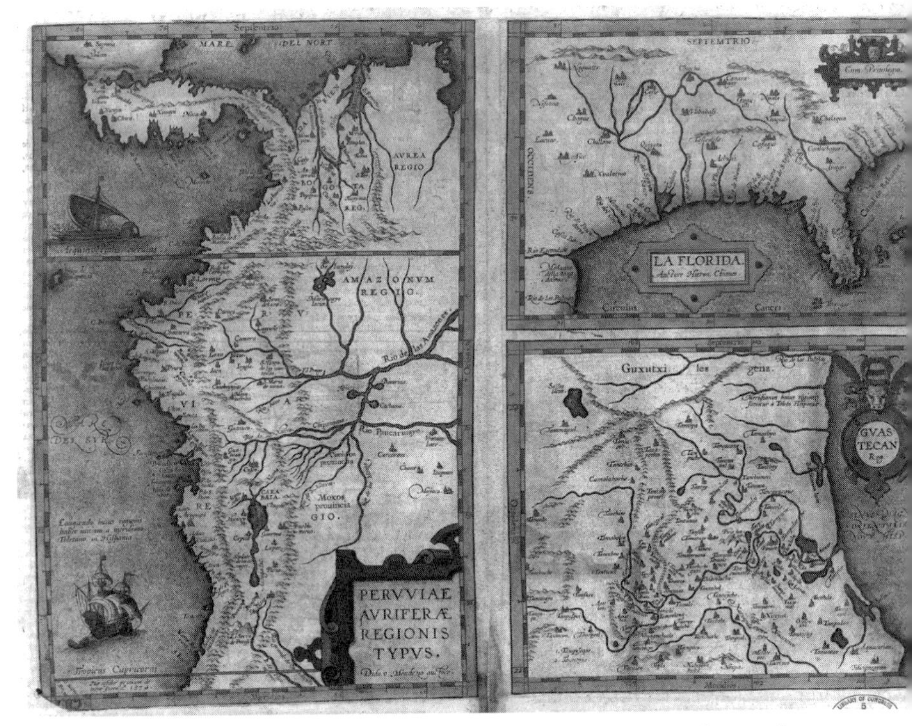

Ortelius, *La Florida,* 1584. Abraham Ortelius, a Flemish cartographer, made these three maps of North and South America in 1584. The one in the upper right shows La Florida as all of the present-day southeastern United States. (Courtesy of University of Nebraska, Omaha.)

replica shelter such as those used by the Timucua. Outside the fort is a replica outdoor oven. The triangular fort itself is surrounded on two sides by a small moat and by raised wooden walls. Cannons on display inside the fort give a sense of the types of defenses that might have been used. The fort commands a nice view over the river. There are no structures inside the fort walls.

Things to See Nearby

Less than a half mile to the east of the park entrance is a marked entrance to the parking lot for a replica concrete column, representing the stone column placed by Jean Ribault to mark the claim of France to the region. Ribault's workers built the original monument on a nearby site, not yet precisely located, on May 2, 1562.

Thirty-five miles to the south is St. Augustine, with the Castillo de San Marcos, and 15 miles farther south, at the tip of Anastasia Island, is Fort Matanzas. The Kingsley Plantation, located in the Timucuan Ecological and Historic Preserve, off SR 105 north of the St. Johns River, is open daily. A few locales of U.S. Civil War skirmishes are located within the Ecological Preserve, and directions to them can be obtained at the visitor center.

History

The histories of Fort Caroline, near Jacksonville, and of the founding of St. Augustine, are closely tied together. The two settlements grew out of the furious, but little-remembered 1560s conflict between France and Spain for control of Florida, and through Florida, control of trade routes to what is now the continental United States. And French troops from Fort Caroline were slaughtered at the site of Fort Matanzas.

The settlement at Fort Caroline came about as an effort by France to settle Protestant Huguenots in the New World, a very early indication of the role that religious intolerance and religious toleration would play in the settlements that became the United States. Charles IX became king of France at age ten, in 1560. His mother, Catherine de Medici, supported the plans of Admiral Gaspart de Coligny, a prominent Huguenot, to settle other Huguenots in North America, as a way to escape the growing persecution of Protestants by Roman Catholics in France. The first of a number of massacres in France of French Huguenots occurred in 1562, despite the monarchy's insistence on a policy of moderation. With support from Charles and the admiral, a small exploratory expedition led by the Norman sailor Jean Ribault (1520–65) left for the New World in 1562.

Reaching the Florida coast, Ribault found an inlet and river that he named the River of May, the present-day St. Johns River, and erected a stone monument claiming the land for France. The concrete pillar erected by the Daughters of the American

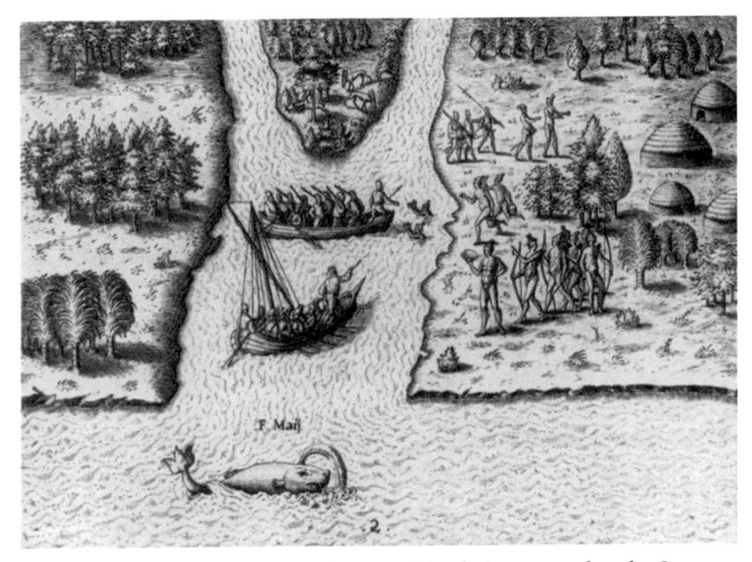

When the French expedition under Jean Ribault first arrived at the St. Johns River, they named it the River of May, commemorating their arrival in that month. (1591 engraving by Theodor de Bry, after a watercolor by Jacques Le Moyne. Courtesy of the Library of Congress.)

Revolution commemorates this stone marker on a bluff overlooking the river, just to the east of the Fort Caroline replica site in the Timucua Ecological and Historic Preserve.

After erecting the marker, Ribault sailed north and established a small settlement of twenty-eight men in what is now South Carolina, on Parris Island in Port Royal Sound, known as Charlesfort. However, the garrison there soon gave up, and all but one of the soldiers sailed for France in a small open boat. Their bad luck continued as they ran out of food and the survivors resorted to cannibalism. An English ship finally rescued them in English waters. Meanwhile, Ribault himself had been detained by the English. In France, a second expedition—led by Ribault's second in command, René Goulaine de Laudonnière—with two hundred soldiers and artisans, including a few women, left France in April 1564, to try again.

Laudonnière and settlers located Ribault's monument on the St. Johns River, and on June 22, 1564, they began building a settlement and fort. They named the territory "La Caroline" after

King Charles. At first, the local Timucua Native Americans were curious and supportive, trading food with the settlers and quietly observing the construction. Outside the present replica of the fort, on the trail leading to it from the visitor center, one can see a small display of a native shelter, intended to demonstrate how the Timucua watched the work from a respectful distance.

The initial warm welcome by the Timucua inhabitants soon vanished, however, and by the next spring, the French settlers ran low on food. At least two small mutinous parties sailed off for the Caribbean, where some were captured by the Spanish. Questioning revealed the fact that they had come from a settlement in Florida. By the summer of 1565, the settlers were ready to abandon the little colony and return to France. In the meantime, in June 1565, the English had released Ribault. On his return to France, Admiral Coligny put Ribault in charge of a relief expedition to head for La Caroline. Ribault sailed with supplies and some six hundred more soldiers and settlers, arriving in August 1565.

In this 1591 engraving, the Timucua venerate a column erected by Jean Ribault during the first French expedition to Florida. A replica of the monument overlooking the St. Johns River can be visited today. (Theodor de Bry, after a watercolor by Jacques Le Moyne. Courtesy of the Library of Congress.)

This small shelter on the grounds of Fort Caroline depicts the position of Timucua Native Americans as they watched the French construct the fort. (Loretta Carlisle photo.)

The Spanish decided to enforce their claims to Florida, and the newly appointed Spanish governor, Don Pedro Menéndez de Avilés, led a force to dislodge the French outpost. After a brief skirmish, the French ships drove off Menéndez, who retreated south. He established his first settlement at what later became St. Augustine. Ribault chased after the retreating Spanish with a fleet and several hundred troops. A turning point in history followed.

A storm battered the French fleet during the short voyage south along the coast. It may have been a hurricane, as the ships wrecked in October, in the midst of the hurricane season along this coast. Many of the men died at sea, and the survivors struggled ashore, some landing near what is now Daytona and others farther south toward Cape Canaveral.

Menéndez led a Spanish force estimated to be about five hundred, which marched the 35 miles northward overland from St. Augustine to Fort Caroline and, in a dawn attack, overwhelmed the small defending French force at the fort, where some 200 to 250 soldiers and settlers remained, including women and children. The Spanish troops slaughtered the soldiers, sparing only

The replica of Fort Caroline is about ⅓ scale; thus this moat is much smaller than the original moat around the exterior wooden walls. (Loretta Carlisle photo.)

The stockade at Fort Caroline, from inside the fort, shows the high wall facing the water side and the earthen firing positions guarding the land approaches. (Loretta Carlisle photo.)

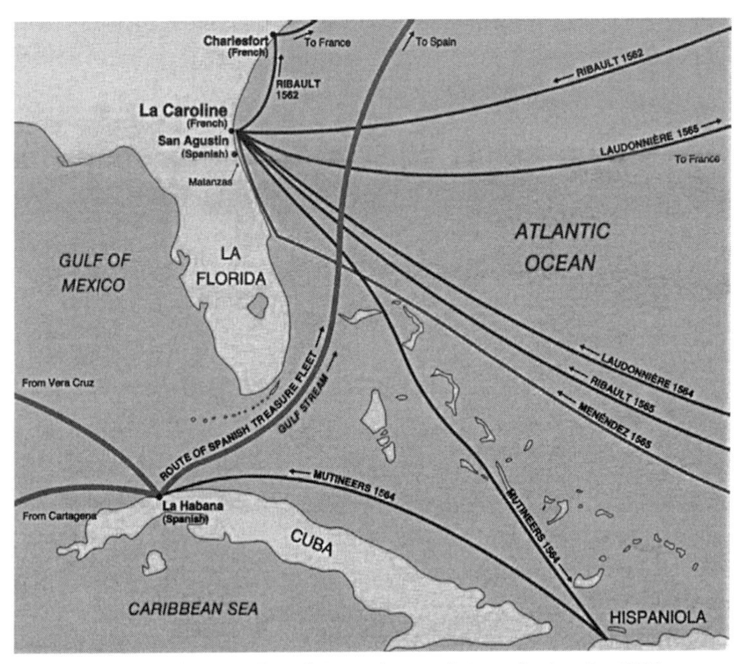

Routes taken by the French and Spanish expeditions during the 1560s conflicts. (National Park Service map.)

some of the women and children. Laudonnière escaped with some forty to fifty men, but the Spanish executed the fort's defenders on the spot.

After returning to St. Augustine, Menéndez learned of the group of survivors from Ribault's fleet, some 15 miles to the south on the shore facing the southern end of Anastasia Island. Menéndez's troops marched out and confronted the shipwrecked troops. Menéndez located some 127 Frenchmen who had marched overland as far as the inlet. Since they were starving, they surrendered. Menéndez demanded that they renounce their Protestant faith and accept Catholicism, but they refused. The Spanish soldiers axed 111 Frenchmen to death on September 29, 1565, sparing only sixteen: some few who proclaimed their Catholic faith, some Breton sailors, and four artisans needed to work at St. Augustine. Two weeks later, another group of

French survivors reached the inlet, including Jean Ribault. On October 12, Ribault and his men surrendered, again refusing to give up their Protestant faith. This time, the Spanish killed 134. From that time, the inlet bore the name "Matanzas"—meaning "slaughters" in Spanish, for the two separate massacres.

Although later generations viewed the killings as horrible, to keep the tragedy in proportion, it should be remembered that in the same era in France, civil conflict between Catholics and Huguenots had led to far more massive slaughters of Huguenots, including estimates of two thousand in Paris, and more than six thousand elsewhere in France in 1572. In this so-called St. Bartholomew's Day Massacre in France, Catholics killed Admiral Coligny himself, along with many other prominent Huguenot leaders.

In the 1740s, the Spanish constructed a fort near the massacre site: "Fort Matanzas" protected the approaches to St. Augustine from British ships entering the bay from the south.

It is interesting to consider, in regard to this historic turning point, that if the French troops had delayed their departure from Fort Caroline by a few days, avoiding the heavy storm that battered the coast, they would have been strong enough in numbers to have overwhelmed the Spanish at their partially completed fortification at St. Augustine. Had the French captured that port, it is possible that Florida would have been a French colony, not a Spanish one, for the next two hundred years or more.

At Fort Caroline, the Spanish occupied the fort, which later burned, probably accidentally. They later constructed their own fortification near or on the same spot. The French retaliated for the earlier slaughter, in 1568, when Dominique de Gourgues led an attack that captured the fort once again. In retribution of the massacre at Matanzas, de Gourgues slaughtered the surrendering Spanish troops at the fort. After his departure, the Spanish rebuilt the fort, but then abandoned it permanently. The present replica is a two-thirds scale modern construction that follows illustrations by Jacques le Moyne, done as an engraving by Theodor de Bry. The le Moyne and de Bry illustrations of the

Native Americans of Florida were among the first depictions of the peoples who inhabited North America ever seen in Europe, and they were widely reproduced.

During the American Civil War, troops fought several skirmishes in lands now included in and near the Timucua Ecological and Historic Preserve, and the city of Jacksonville itself changed hands several times during the war. Noted encounters took place at St. Johns Bluff, Yellow Bluff, and Cedar Point. The skirmish at St. Johns Bluff took place in what is now the Fort Caroline National Memorial. Directions to the other sites can be found at the visitor center of the Fort Caroline National Memorial.

President Truman named Fort Caroline as a National Memorial on September 21, 1950; it was established on January 16, 1953. Together with the Theodore Roosevelt nature area, it is administered as the Timucuan Ecological and Historic Preserve.

11

Fort Mose

Location: 2 miles north of St. Augustine.
Driving Directions: Turn east from US 1 at the New City Gates (marked by statues of conquistadors) on Fort Mose Trail, which dead-ends into the parking and picnic areas of the Fort Mose State Park.
Hours of Operation: Visitor center: 9 a.m. to 5 p.m., Thursday through Monday. Park grounds: 8 a.m. to sundown, Thursday through Monday. Closed Tuesday and Wednesday.
Fees: $4 per vehicle (limit 8 people per vehicle). There is an honor box to pay fees; correct change is required. $2 for pedestrians, bicyclists, extra passengers, passengers in vehicle with holder of Annual Individual Entrance Pass.
Phone: (904) 823-2232

Unique Facts

Fort Mose (pronounced "Mo-Say") is the first known, legally sanctioned, self-governing community of free blacks in what is now the United States. It represents the historically oldest site on Florida's Black Heritage Trail. However, the actual locale of the forts and settlements are now only archaeological dig sites.

Things to See

An orientation film about 20 minutes long provides a thumbnail history of Fort Mose. Exhibits inside the visitor center include

The visitor center at Fort Mose commemorates this first free African American community in what is now the continental United States. (Loretta Carlisle photo.)

a developing display showing the history of the fort; with displays of archaeological finds at the site, and art done by visiting children.

A wooden gangplank into the marsh leads to a viewing platform from which the original sites of Fort Mose can be seen. From the boardwalk, there are fine opportunities for photographing seabirds. The archaeological sites of the original forts are not accessible to the general public.

Things to See Nearby

The marshland surrounding the walkway and in front of the viewing platform is a beautiful example of Florida's tidal marshes, inhabited by numerous wildfowl. Take along binoculars and a good camera, and then look toward the pine trees at the rookery to see the great blue heron nests. Other birds typically sighted at the rookery and from the boardwalk include snowy egrets, wood storks, tri-colored herons, and white ibises.

Nearby military sites of interest are Castillo de San Marcos in Saint Augustine, Fort Matanzas at the southern tip of Anastasia

Island, and the coquina quarry on Anastasia Island. St. Augustine, the oldest European-established city in the continental United States, is itself a major visitor attraction, with numerous historic sites.

The defenses of St. Augustine were later strengthened by the construction of an outer defensive wall that crossed the peninsula, with Fort Mose the wall's eastern extremity. The current "new gates" on the highway mark the location of this outer defensive wall. The wall and Fort Mose represented a northern perimeter that could be defended against attacks by British forces coming from the colonies to the north down the San Juan Road. The wall, sometimes called the Mose Wall, represented the first line of defense of St. Augustine. Another line lay about halfway between the Mose Line and the Castillo, about where Myrtle Avenue is now, a classic example of defense-in-depth then current in Europe. To the west of St. Augustine, another line, known as the Pupa Line, anchored on Fort St. Francis de Pupa (near the St. Johns River), provided still more protection for the city. Castillo de San Marcos itself is located on the seaward end of an inner city wall of St. Augustine (the Cubo Line) that ran a few blocks along present-day Orange Street to the San Sebastian River to the west,

Fort Mose was built on a site now surrounded by marsh and marked by this clump of trees. Archaeological work at the site has uncovered many clues about life at the fort. (Loretta Carlisle photo.)

showing how both forts and the various fortified lines served as part of the defense of the city. Maps of the era clearly show Fort Mose strategically located near the road from the north, as part of the outer defensive perimeter to the north of St. Augustine.

History

Although most U.S. history textbooks tend to downplay the struggle for freedom by African Americans themselves, Florida has many examples of the little-known "*other* Underground Railroad" or escape route for slaves from the American South, which headed to refuges with the Spanish and with the Seminole Indians. This southerly escape route existed long before the American Revolution, and continued in one form or another up until the Civil War in 1861–65. Fort Mose shows that the roots of this southern pathway to freedom go well back into the Spanish period.

The Spanish ruled Florida during the colonial period (1560s–1763), and after an interlude of British government, the Spanish held Florida again in the period 1783–1821. In the first period, the Spanish could not afford to place large garrisons of troops in Florida, and relied on the strong fort at Castillo de San Marcos in St. Augustine to protect the Spanish settlements from invasion by British forces, either by sea or overland from the British colonies of Georgia and the Carolinas. To strengthen those defenses, the Spanish encouraged runaway African and African American slaves from the British colonies to come to Florida. If the runaways would accept the Catholic religion, they would be offered their freedom.

Some of the freedom seekers settled under the protection of Castillo de San Marcos, finding employment in construction and in the town. An estimated one hundred free Africans had settled in St. Augustine by 1738. Governor Manuel de Montiano set aside some vacant Indian lands just two miles north of the Castillo, with the idea that the Africans could build their own community and fort there that would serve as an outer line of

Displays inside the Fort Mose visitor center depict daily life in this free African American community under Spanish rule. (Loretta Carlisle photo.)

defense for the town of St. Augustine and for Castillo de San Marcos.

Any gunfight there could serve as an alarm or "trip-wire," alerting the fort and town to prepare. At the site, the black refugees from slavery built a small walled village, with a church and pointed fort bastion walls facing inland from the waterway.

There were two forts at Mose. The first fort had a square shape, with corner bastions. During the brief "War of Jenkins' Ear" fought in 1739–40, Fort Mose played a crucial role in the struggle between the British and Spanish for control of Florida. English colonists from Georgia established militias who marched with regular British troops under Governor James Oglethorpe. As they moved slowly overland, scouts brought back word of their advance, and Governor Montiano evacuated the residents and black troops from Fort Mose, bringing them into the safety of Castillo de San Marcos. The British troops under Oglethorpe, numbering some 137 men, carrying muskets, occupied the abandoned black fort.

Two days after the British had occupied Fort Mose, on June 26, 1740, the black militia and Spanish troops, numbering about three hundred altogether, marched north, quietly ambushing the British at 4:00 a.m. Some of the British left their dead and hastily evacuated, running north, with the legend of the attack at "bloody Moosa" becoming part of Georgia lore. The Spanish reported taking thirty-four prisoners, leaving sixty-eight British dead. The Spanish commended the black militia captain, Francisco Menéndez, for his bravery and leadership in the surprise attack. Menéndez, born in Africa of Mandingo ancestry, had fled Georgia in 1724, before rising to his position of leadership in the African militia of Fort Mose. The Spanish troops, black militia, and Native American warriors destroyed the fort, so that it could not be reused by the British. The Spanish and their black allies never rebuilt that fort.

Oglethorpe continued to try to subdue Castillo de San Marcos, but it remained impregnable. When Spanish reinforcements arrived from Cuba, Oglethorpe and the remnants of his troops marched back to Georgia.

Over the next years, the black members of the Spanish militia continued to serve, and later rebuilt the town and village at Fort Mose to the northeast of the first site in the 1750s. The second fort had three sides, with a fourth side open to the water; it had a moat and two corner bastions. Later rising waters have isolated the spot in the midst of a marsh. The settlers named the new community "Gracia Real de Santa Theresa de Mose."

By 1752, Mose had become a thriving settlement again, with an estimated population running up to one hundred over the next decade or so. The settlers not only farmed the land there, but hunted deer and other game, fished in the local waters, and worked as sailors, cow hunters, construction workers, blacksmiths, and at other jobs in St. Augustine.

However, at the end of the Seven Years' War in 1763, Spain ceded all of Florida to Britain. To ensure the safety of the African Americans, to prevent their being reenslaved and taken back to Georgia, all of the Fort Mose population evacuated to Cuba. In Cuba, they established a small settlement known as Ceiba Mocha.

Accurate Map of the West Indies drawn in 1740 by British mapmaker Emanuel Bowen. It shows the contemporary strategic position of Florida in relation to the West Indies. (Courtesy of the Library of Congress.)

That town is still there, about 20 miles east of Havana. The black settlers abandoned Fort Mose, and it fell into ruin as the waters of the marsh rose gradually and the damming of the creeks by the Vilano Bridge and embankment inundated the small plots of farmland and the fort itself.

Historians knew little of the story of the first fort site until the mid-1980s, although the second village, built in the 1750s, remained a popular spot to visit and fish. In 1986–88, a team of historians and archaeologists headed by Dr. Kathleen Deagan of the Florida Museum of Natural History conducted a thorough investigation of the site at Fort Mose, uncovering many artifacts. Together with documentary evidence from Spanish records, the team of historians and archaeologists pieced the story together. In the digs, they found bullets, weapon parts, buttons and buckles from uniforms, clay pipes, and household items. Archaeologists uncovered the remains of the original fort itself, including the moat, the clay-covered earth walls, and evidence of the wooden buildings inside the fort. Ordinary items from daily life helped tell the story of life there, including thimbles, nails, ceramics, and glass bottles. A hand-made St. Christopher's medal attested to the fact of the Catholic conversion of the settlers there.

Historical research into documents in the colonial archives in Spain turned up more specific facts. Dr. Jane Landers uncovered the names of some of those who lived in Mose and something about their way of life. She established that by 1759, the village consisted of twenty-two palm thatch huts. The population then included sixty-seven people: thirty-seven men, fifteen women, seven boys, and eight girls. The settlers attended Mass in a wooden church that also housed the priest. The fugitives from Georgia and Carolina married fellow escapees, but some married Native Americans or slaves or free Africans already living in St. Augustine.

The National Register of Historic Places listed the site in 1994, and it is now included in the Florida Black Heritage Trail documentation. The site is administered by the Florida State Park Service.

12

Castillo de San Marcos (Fort San Marcos)

Location: 1 South Castillo Drive, St. Augustine.
Directions: From I-95, take the exit for "St. Augustine Historic Sites and Downtown" (SR 16, exit 318). Follow SR 16 to US 1. Turn right on US 1 and go 2 miles to Castillo Drive. Turn left on Castillo Drive; turn right at the traffic light. The Castillo and parking are ahead on the left.
Hours of Operation: 8:45 a.m. to 5:15 p.m. daily. Closed Christmas. (The ticket booth closes at 4:45 p.m.) The park grounds are closed from midnight until 5:30 a.m.
Fees: Adults (16 and older), $6, pass valid for 7 days; children (15 and under), no admission charge but must be accompanied by an adult. National Parks and Federal Recreational Lands Passes are accepted.
Phone: (904) 829-6506, ext. 234

Unique Facts

"Oldest"

The Castillo de San Marcos is the oldest masonry fort and the only surviving seventeenth-century fort in North America. The Canadians might challenge this claim since the walls of Old Quebec were built in 1608, but Quebec was not exactly a fort; it is probably more accurately described as a "walled city." A Canadian

These corner towers on the walls of the fort provided excellent fields of fire against any attacking troops. (Loretta Carlisle photo.)

masonry fort, Fort Louisbourg in Nova Scotia, built between 1720 and 1740, ranks as one of the oldest on the continent. Another challenge might come from Puerto Rico. Overlooking the entrance to San Juan harbor in Puerto Rico, Morro Castle (El Castillo San Felipe del Morro) can lay claim to being older since part of it was built in 1589. So to be strictly correct, it has to be stated that Castillo de San Marcos in Florida is the oldest masonry fort on the *mainland* of North America, north of Mexico.

Unique Construction

An unusual feature of the fort is the fact it was built from coquina, a sedimentary stone built up from the deposit of seashells. To build the fort, workers quarried, cured, and then transported the coquina by water from Anastasia Island, across the bay from St. Augustine. Coquina is not entirely unique to Castillo de San

Marcos, as the Spanish also used it in the construction of some other structures in the region, including private homes.

Five Flags

While a number of forts and locations in the United States can claim to have been under several flags, Castillo de San Marcos really did have five flags legitimately flown over it in the course of its history. The flags were: Spain 1672–1763; Britain 1763–81; Spain again 1763–1821; the United States of America 1821–61; the sovereign state of Florida, January 1861–February 1861; the Confederate States of America, February 1861–March 1862, and the United States again since March 1862. Not counting repetitions, the changes of authority meant that over its long history, the fort operated under five separate flags and military/governing powers.

Guarding the "Oldest City"

The fort guards over the city and harbor of St. Augustine, the oldest continuously occupied European-established city in the continental United States, first settled in 1565. San Juan, Puerto Rico, founded in 1521, predates St. Augustine, so the point must be made that St. Augustine is the oldest in the *continental* United States. Taos Pueblo in New Mexico has been continuously occupied since at least 1450 CE. Of course, Native Americans built and occupied Taos Pueblo, not Europeans. Thus it is accurate to say that Castillo de San Marcos guards the oldest continuously occupied *European-established* city in the continental United States. There are several cities in Mexico and Central America that predate St. Augustine, Florida.

Four Wars, Never Conquered

Although Castillo de San Marcos survived several attacks and at least six very bloody wars that raged around it, the fort never surrendered under fire. It stood through sieges during Queen

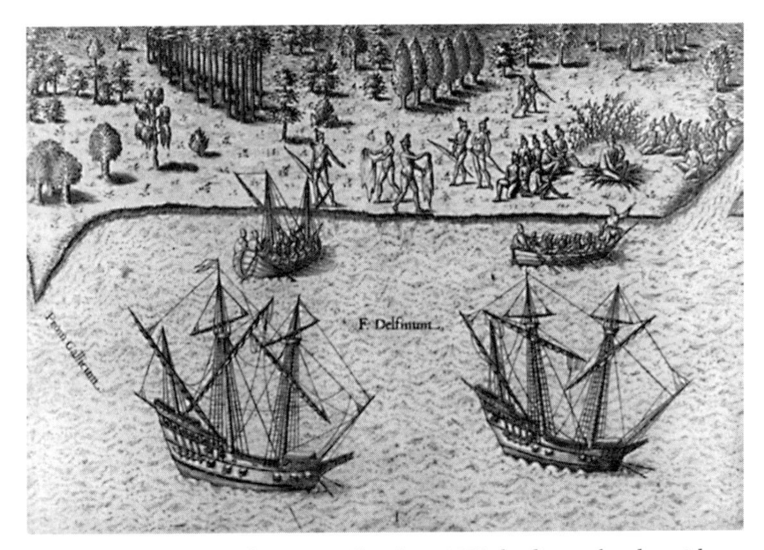

The French set up a settlement in Florida in 1562, leading to battles with the Spanish. This 16th-century engraving depicts the first French landing on the Florida coast. (Theodor de Bry after a watercolor by Jacques Le Moyne. Courtesy of the Library of Congress.)

Anne's War (1701–13) and the War of Jenkins' Ear (1739–48); Spain peacefully transferred the fort to England at the end of the Seven Years' War (1756–63); England transferred the fort back, again in a peaceful ceremony, to Spain at the end of the War of American Independence (1776–83); after the war of 1812 (1812–15) Spain ceded Florida and the fort to the United States under the Adams-Onis Treaty of 1821; during the American Civil War, the United States peacefully transferred the fort from U.S. control to Florida; Florida turned the fort over to the Confederacy in 1861; U.S. troops peacefully regained control in 1862.

Things to See

Aside from the magnificent overall view of the Castillo from outside, special things to notice and see include the following:

- Coquina construction blocks with the unique, locally quarried mortar (from crushed and baked oyster shells)

- Rooms converted to prison quarters surrounding the central courtyard or plaza
- The ramp from the plaza to the upper tier, built so that heavy guns could be drawn up to position by mules
- The view over the harbor and of the city of St. Augustine from the battlements on the upper level
- The display of bronze and iron guns mounted on the upper (terreplein) level

Some of the guns on display were not contemporaneous with the Spanish era of the fort, but were captured in Cuba during the Spanish-American War in 1898.

The fort provides a fine opportunity to see some construction features used in forts and castles of the seventeenth and eighteenth centuries.

The fort has four nearly equal triangular-shaped corners. They were known as St. Peter, St. Paul, St. Augustine, and St. Charles. The four tall outside walls are known as curtains or curtain walls. Three of the corners have round, protruding sentry towers known

On the roof, or terreplein, of Castillo de San Marcos is a display of numerous cannon, some captured from Spain during the Spanish-American War of 1898. (Loretta Carlisle photo.)

as bastions. On the northeast corner, there is a high watchtower with a view over both land and harbor approaches. The curtain walls are about 15 feet thick at the base, tapering to about 9 feet at the top, and the walls are about 33 feet high.

The plaza, or inner court, is a square about 100 feet on each side. Almost all the casemates or rooms built into the walls open into the plaza. Altogether there are 26 casemates. In addition, there are five windowless rooms and one magazine for powder storage.

The only entrance is through a sally port or gate in the middle of the south curtain wall, facing toward downtown St. Augustine.

The roof over the space between the inner and outer walls, the "terreplein," is about 40 feet wide. A number of guns were mounted on the terreplein, surrounded by a 6-foot-high, 3-foot-thick wall or parapet. Some 64 slots in the parapet allowed placement of guns. The parapet that looks over the harbor is a bit lower than the parapets on the other sides of the terreplein.

Defenders in the sentry towers had an excellent view of any attackers on two sides, and could shoot firearms or arrows from the narrow slits or loopholes in the towers while being quite protected from enemy missiles. Behind the fort is a hot-shot oven for heating cannonballs to red-hot heat before firing them at enemy ships.

From the outside of the fort or from the parapet, the visitor gets a good view of the berm and moat; the outer earthen mound, known as a rampart; and the sloped supporting buttresses that merge into the wall, known as pilaster buttresses. At the sally port, a small drawbridge that could be raised helped prevent attackers from getting inside.

One of the features of coquina is that it can absorb impact. When struck by a cannonball, the ball would penetrate and lodge in the wall, with the coquina absorbing the shot rather than splintering or shattering like other types of rock. So this building material, used because laborers could dig it locally and because more solid stone could not be found in the required amount, turned out to be an excellent construction material for a fort.

This oven was used to heat cannonballs until they were red-hot, so that when fired against enemy ships attacking St. Augustine, they would ignite the ship or set off its gunpowder. The hot-shot oven sits outside the fort on the east side. (Loretta Carlisle photo.)

The architecture and coquina construction help explain why Castillo de San Marcos withstood several attacks and was never defeated in battle, but only surrendered peacefully under treaties or other agreements. And those facts explain why it is here today, the only fort of its era surviving on the continent of North America, north of Mexico.

Things to See Nearby

City Gate

Across Castillo Drive and in view of the entrance to the Castillo are the sentry towers that bordered the city gate of St. Augustine. Also built of coquina, and also under the jurisdiction of the National Park Service, the towers of the gateway mark the main land entrance to the city of St. Augustine. Through the gate towers, in a few square blocks easily walked (or toured by wheelchair), is Old St. Augustine.

Old St. Augustine

This bustling little shopping and residential section boasts a main street (St. George) that is pedestrian-only, lined with shops, restaurants, with a number of historic buildings identified with markers. Among the historic structures in Old St. Augustine is the González-Alvarez House at 14 St. Francis Street. It is the oldest surviving Spanish colonial dwelling in Florida (not the oldest in the United States). The spot has been occupied since the 1600s, while the present structure dates from the early 1700s. Visitors have toured the house since 1893, where they can see displays and material documenting the Spanish, British, and American occupations of St. Augustine. The U.S. Department of the Interior designated the house a National Historic Landmark in 1973, and the house is owned and operated by the St. Augustine Historical Society. Admission is $8 for adults, $7 for seniors and military personnel, and $4 for students; family admission is $18. Old St. Augustine contains many other points of historic interest:

- Dow Museum of Historic Houses: nine historic homes dating from 1790 to 1910
- Flagler College: the former Hotel Ponce de Leon built by Henry Flagler in 1887
- Lightner Museum: antiques from America's Gilded Age
- Mission Nombre de Dios: America's first mission and site of the founding of St. Augustine in 1565
- Old Jail: built by Henry Flagler in 1891 and listed on the National Register of Historic Places
- Oldest Wooden Schoolhouse: originally a residence, converted to a schoolhouse
- Saint Photios Greek Orthodox National Shrine: Dedicated to the first settlement of Greek people in the United States, circa 1768
- Spanish Military Hospital: Spanish medicine in colonial times

Among the many historic sites near Castillo de San Marcos in St. Augustine is the oldest wooden schoolhouse in the United States. (Loretta Carlisle photo.)

- St. Augustine Lighthouse: 165 feet above sea level
- Villa Zorayda Museum: elegant Gilded Age home built by Franklin W. Smith in 1883
- Colonial Spanish Quarter: a museum representing 1740s St. Augustine
- Old Coquina Quarry Site: immediately across the Bridge of Lions, in the Anastasia State Park. A marked trail leads to the Old Coquina Quarry Site, where laborers mined the building material for Castillo de San Marcos.

Nearby forts whose history intersects with that of Castillo de San Marcos:

- Fort Mose (2.2 miles north), p. 99
- Fort Matanzas (14 miles south), p. 127
- Fort Clinch (56 miles north), p. 76

The coquina, or natural cement, mined from this quarry on nearby Anastasia Island made an excellent building material for Castillo de San Marcos. (Loretta Carlisle photo.)

History

The Early Fort

The Spanish founded and settled the city of St. Augustine in 1565. Francis Drake, the English privateer operating under commission from Queen Elizabeth I, led a fleet that attacked and destroyed the town of St. Augustine in June 1586. The attack served as a warning that the fort at St. Augustine needed to be strengthened. Workers soon surrounded the original wooden fort with a newly dug moat, reinforced the outer, or curtain, walls and built new casemates or gun-mount chambers.

The final construction out of coquina began in 1672. The coquina came from the quarry on nearby Anastasia Island, where it was cut in blocks and cured. Slaves and prisoners would carry the heavy blocks, suspended between iron poles. Sometimes with the help of oxen teams, they carried the blocks over a causeway to Quarry Creek, where waiting barges tied up, ready to transport the blocks to the fort site. On Anastasia Island, Old Quarry Road and Coquina Avenue are named to memorialize the ancient quarry site, which is located inside Anastasia State Park, right off the parking area just inside the entrance to the park.

At the fort, experienced masons from Cuba placed the coquina blocks, using a mortar that they made on-site. They crushed oyster shells, baked them until nearly pure lime remained, then mixed the lime with water to form an excellent "tabby" mortar that more than three hundred years later still holds the coquina blocks securely in place.

The fort endured a number of attacks and sieges from English privateers and pirates. Attackers burned the city of Saint Augustine (either partially or entirely) at least ten times, but the Castillo de San Marcos never fell during the attacks and often provided a refuge for the city's residents and officials. St. Augustine served as the capital of Florida under the Spanish. The Castillo de San Marcos and several lines of defensive works protected the city on the north and west from possible land attack from the British colonies; the fort also guarded the harbor against attacks

Map of St. Augustine and vicinity, 1595, showing the first wooden fortress that preceded the Castillo de San Marcos in guarding the town. Original in the *Archivo General de Indias*, Seville, Spain. (Courtesy of the Library of Congress.)

from the sea. The city was a "presidio," or seat of a presiding governor, supported by troops.

British Threats

Despite the strong defenses, the British attacked the Spanish settlement a number of times. Sailing from Charleston, South Carolina (founded in 1670), a British expedition threatened St. Augustine in 1702 during Queen Anne's War. Some 1,200 residents of St. Augustine took refuge inside the Castillo, while the raiding British burned the city. The British cannons, however, were ineffective against the coquina walls of the Castillo. When Spanish ships arrived to rescue the city, the British burned their own ships and retreated overland to the North. Following that attack, the Spanish rebuilt the fort and the city, strengthening defenses by 1738.

War of Jenkins' Ear (1739–48)

St. Augustine and Castillo de San Marcos suffered another attack during the War of Jenkins' Ear. This oddly named war began with an international incident on the open seas. On April 9, 1731, the Spanish patrol sloop *San Antonio* intercepted near Havana, Cuba, a British merchant brig, the *Rebecca*. That brig had sailed from Jamaica, bound for London. The Spanish authorities examined the brig's papers and cargo, finding some inconsistencies, suggesting the ship was engaged in smuggling into Spanish colonies. According to the Spanish account of the incident, Captain Robert Jenkins verbally insulted the Spanish captain, Juan de Leon Fandino. Indignant that his honor as an officer had been affronted, Fandino took his sword and cut off one of Jenkins's ears. According to Jenkins's account, Fandino added insult to injury by stating, "Were the King of England here and also in violation of the laws, I would do the same for him!"

Jenkins made his way back to England, and in 1738, testifying before a committee of the House of Commons, Jenkins gave his report of the incident and actually produced his preserved ear. Jenkins claimed not only that Fandino severed his ear and insulted the British Crown, but that Fandino's men stole goods from the *Rebecca,* seized the crew, and set the vessel adrift. Hearing the news and Jenkins's report, the British public demanded retribution. The resulting war pitted the new British colony of Georgia (which had been founded in 1733), against the long-standing Spanish colony in Florida.

Gen. James Oglethorpe, one of the founders of the colony of Georgia, had prior military experience and had served as a member of Parliament. He first shipped to Georgia in 1733 with thirty-five families of settlers, hoping to establish a refuge for debtors in Britain. With the outbreak of war in 1739, Oglethorpe prepared for an assault on the Spanish holdings in Florida. With a force of two thousand, about half of them Native Americans, he made several passes into the Spanish colony in January 1740, seizing two outlying forts, Picolata and San Francis de Pupa, that lay to the north and west of St. Augustine on opposite banks of the St. Johns River. He overran Fort Mose, and the black troops and settlers there fled south to St. Augustine and Castillo de San Marcos. By May, Oglethorpe was ready for an assault on the Castillo itself, but problems with the diverse militias under his command ruined any chance for a surprise attack.

He launched a siege against the fort, but without coordination of land and sea forces, he had to pull out by July 1740, falling back to Fort Frederica, where he set up defenses against an expected Spanish counterattack. Black troops fighting for the Spanish under Francisco Menéndez recaptured Fort Mose.

The full Spanish counterattack came in the summer of 1742. After a couple of skirmishes, the Spanish retreated back to St. Augustine, and Oglethorpe planned another attack on the Castillo in March 1743. That assault failed, and represented the last land battle of the War of Jenkins' Ear. Five years later, Britain and Spain signed the Treaty of Aix-la-Chappelle, recognizing each other's colonial claims and agreeing on the St. Johns River as the boundary between Florida and Georgia.

British Period, 1764–81, Fort St. Marks

The British took over Castillo de San Marcos peacefully in 1764. In that year, after the settlement of the Seven Years' War (1756–63), Britain acquired all of Florida in exchange for returning Havana, Cuba, to Spain, which the British had captured during that war. Many of the Spanish colonists and all the government officials in Florida left, turning over the small garrison towns of St. Augustine and Pensacola to the British. The British renamed Castillo de San Marcos as Fort St. Marks, and they divided Florida into East and West Florida. The British ruled East Florida from St. Augustine, and West Florida from a separate capital, Pensacola.

During the American Revolution, or War for Independence, 1775–83, the British colonies of Florida remained loyal. West Florida, sometimes known as the "Fourteenth Colony," did not send delegates to the Continental Congress, although invited to do so. The Spanish entered the war on the side of the American Patriots in 1779. In May 1781, the Spanish retook Pensacola. At the end of the war in 1783, under the Paris Peace Treaty, Spain regained control of the rest of Florida. During the war, no shots had been fired at Castillo de San Marcos (or Fort St. Marks, as the British called it), and it changed flags from Spain to Britain and back to Spain in peaceful ceremonies. The British had done little to maintain the fort.

Spain Again, 1783–1821

Over the next four decades, Spain remained in control of Florida, although increasingly, Native Americans from the Creek tribe and escaped slaves made their way into the colony to escape the advancing European-descended planters and settlers from Georgia and South Carolina who moved westward into what is now western Georgia and Alabama. The Seminoles, as the Native American refugees came to be called, and the African Americans who settled among them lived apart from the Spanish settlements in their own communities, defending their independence by force of arms when necessary. Spain had other problems besides this growing community, however.

A rising tide of independence movements in Spanish America led to a series of revolutions and clashes through the period from the early 1800s to the mid-1820s. By 1821, incursions of troops into West Florida under Andrew Jackson, and the increasing difficulty of maintaining control over the restless empire, led Spain to accept the Adams-Onis Treaty of 1821, under which Spain ceded Florida to the United States. The treaty also set the western boundary between Spanish-held Mexico and the United States.

Once again, in 1821, Castillo de San Marcos changed hands peacefully, this time to the United States of America.

United States, 1821–61

The first U.S. Army garrison stationed in St. Augustine, the Fourth Regiment of Artillery, originally planned to occupy quarters at the southern end of town in facilities known as St. Francis Barracks. But those barracks had fallen into such disrepair that the garrison moved into Castillo de San Marcos, which they called either Fort San Marcos or Fort St. Augustine. By 1825, the U.S. government officially changed the name to Fort Marion, naming it after the leader of irregular forces in South Carolina who fought against the British in the American War of Independence, Gen. Francis Marion, "the Swamp Fox."

Indian Imprisonment

The United States engaged in three wars against the Seminoles in Florida, and Osceola emerged as a natural leader after the Second Seminole War broke out in 1835. Osceola came to represent the pride and resistance of the Seminoles and their African American allies against the encroaching white settlers and the U.S. Army.

When Osceola approached U.S. troops under a flag of truce on October 1, 1837, to open negotiations near St. Augustine, U.S. Gen. Thomas S. Jesup treacherously ordered him taken prisoner. Jesup's troops imprisoned Osceola and several other Seminole leaders at Castillo de San Marcos. More captives arranged to escape, but Osceola, already weakened by disease, became even sicker after being held in the cold, wet prison rooms of the Castillo. The Army moved him to Fort Moultrie, in Charleston harbor, where he died on January 20, 1838.

In 1841–42, the Army installed a number of artillery pieces at water level outside the fort. The Army filled the eastern moat of the fort and mounted the guns on the fill. That emplacement, known as a "water battery," defended the fort and the city against ships approaching in the harbor by being able to fire

In the early twentieth century, Castillo de San Marcos was still called Fort Marion, as this Works Progress Administration (WPA) poster from about 1938 shows. (Courtesy of the Library of Congress.)

directly across the water in a straight shot at any approaching enemy vessels. The hot-shot oven stood (and still stands) behind the water battery.

Civil War Years

The beginning of the American Civil War is usually dated to April 12, 1861, with the firing on Fort Sumter in Charleston harbor. However, the secession of the southern states that formed the Confederacy began a few months earlier, in December 1860. Immediately following the election of Abraham Lincoln, South Carolina announced its secession, making it formal on December 20, 1860. Prior to the formation of the Confederacy in February 1861, South Carolina claimed to be an independent republic.

Over January and February 1861, the states on the Gulf of Mexico and Georgia all took steps toward the same status. Even before state conventions formally declared independence from the United States, state troops took over several federal forts, arsenals, and other facilities such as customs houses, post offices, and small Army outposts. In many cases, military facilities in the South were occupied by very small garrisons (often local officers who resigned their U.S. Army commissions) and easily fell under the control of the seceding state governments. But Florida's Fort Jefferson, on one of the islands in the Dry Tortugas group off Florida, just north and west of Key West in the Gulf of Mexico, remained firmly under Union control. Fort Taylor in Key West and Fort Pickens, guarding Pensacola Bay, also remained in Union hands throughout the war.

On January 3, 1861, delegates to the Florida Secession Convention met in the state capital, Tallahassee, to consider the question of secession. Edmund Ruffin of Virginia arrived to confer with Governor Madison S. Perry and members of the convention. The next day, January 4, 1861, Governor Perry decided to seize Federal properties in Florida. In similar ways, governors in other states somewhat forced the issue of secession by taking executive action before a state convention could formally declare the state seceded. The convention continued to debate secession and listened to recommendations for secession, like those from John C. McGehee, a convinced states'-rights plantation owner from Madison County, and from other secessionists like Edmund Ruffin of Virginia. Finally on January 7, 1861, the convention approved a resolution offered by McQueen Macintosh of Apalachicola declaring the state independent of the United States. The resolution was approved 62–5, and the convention declared immediate secession. The same day, a small garrison of Federal soldiers at Castillo de San Marcos, then known as Fort Marion, surrendered their post to a company of local volunteers without a shot being fired.

The fort remained under state control until the formation of the Confederacy on February 4, 1861. Thus for the period of about three weeks after January 7, 1861, the fort flew the flag of the independent state of Florida, until Florida became a state of the Confederate States of America. A year later, however, the fort returned to Union control.

Union ships approached on March 8–10, 1862, without firing a shot, and noted the presence of the strong water battery that had been installed in 1842. The sailors observed the guns without coming ashore. Southern troops did not leave until the night of March 10. The next day, March 11, the USS *Wabash* steamed into the harbor. Sailors rowed an unarmed boat from *Wabash* toward the city with a flag of truce, and at the same time, they spotted a white flag flying above Fort Marion.

To accept the surrender of the fort and the city, Commodore C.R.P. Rodgers met with the mayor and politely informed him that he had come to occupy the city. He told the mayor and other officials that he would respect the private property in the city, and with those assurances, the city and fort were officially surrendered, again without a shot being fired. Rodgers believed that the city harbored many pro-Union sympathizers, although he discovered that the flagstaff in front of the barracks had been cut down, apparently to prevent an official raising of the Union flag. Rumor had it that a group of secession-minded women from the city had cut down the flagpole.

Federal forces acquired not only some good 32-pounder guns from the fort, but also the water battery guns and some antique Spanish guns still mounted at the fort. The fort has remained under the American flag since that time.

Indian Imprisonment: From the Western Indian Wars

In the period 1875–78, as a result of battles in the "Indian Wars" in the United States West, more than ninety-five Native American men, women and children were transported to St. Augustine and held as prisoners in Castillo de San Marcos (Fort Marion). Recent research has identified, by name, thirty-three members of the Cheyenne tribe, twenty-seven Kiowa, eleven Comanche, and scatterings from other groups. Efforts to acculturate the prisoners included religious instruction and training in trades, later conducted at other facilities, such as the Carlisle Indian School in Pennsylvania and at Hampton Institute in Maryland. When these first prisoners moved out, Chiricahua Apaches prisoners, including the followers and family of Geronimo, and other Native American prisoners from the West, replaced them.

During the Spanish-American War in 1898, the Castillo again served as a prison, this time for deserters and mutineers from the U.S. services. That was the last military use of the fort.

In 1900, the military gave up jurisdiction over Fort Marion. In 1924, President Calvin Coolidge designated the fort as a National Monument, and in 1933 the National Park Service took jurisdiction of it from the War Department. The Park Service continued to maintain the fort as a National Monument. In 1942, to recognize its Spanish heritage and construction, the government restored to the fort to its original name of Castillo de San Marcos. The National Register of Historic Places listed the Castillo de San Marcos National Monument on October 15, 1966. The National Park Service manages the Castillo along with Fort Matanzas National Monument. In 1975, the American Society of Civil Engineers formally recognized Castillo de San Marcos as a Historic Civil Engineering Landmark.

13

Fort Matanzas

Location: Off the tip of Anastasia Island, 14 miles south of St. Augustine. The fort itself is located on Rattlesnake Island and is accessible only by ferry; the fort is not handicapped-accessible. Small passenger ferryboats leave a dock just below the visitor center, weather permitting, from 9:30 a.m. to 4:30 p.m.
Driving Directions: From St. Augustine, take the bridge to Anastasia Island; follow Highway A1A South to the end of the island. Follow signs to entrance to the Fort Matanzas National Monument.
Hours of Operation: The visitor center is open from 9:00 a.m. to 4:30 p.m. daily. Closed on Christmas.
Fees: No admission charge.
Phone: (904) 471-0116
Website: www.nps.gov/foma

Unique Facts

"Matanzas" means "massacres" in Spanish, with the fort named after the site where a detachment of 250 to 300 French soldiers, who had departed from Fort Caroline to attack St. Augustine, were shipwrecked and slaughtered by Spanish troops in two separate massacres in 1565. The Spanish built the fort in 1742.

Fort Matanzas National Monument is located at the southern tip of Anastasia Island, on Route A1A. (Loretta Carlisle photo.)

Things to See

The fort is little more than a raised gun platform, with minimal living quarters. The present structure is reconstructed and restored, with an outside staircase for access. Inside, replica cannons and the restored living quarters provide an understanding of how a small detachment of troops could protect St. Augustine from ships approaching from Matanzas Inlet and attempting to sail up the Matanzas River.

Things to See Nearby

Castillo de San Marcos, and St. Augustine, 14 miles north; Fort Mose, 16 miles north; and Fort Caroline, near Jacksonville.

The National Monument area also encloses about 100 acres of natural barrier-island refuge that serves to protect a distinct habitat for a variety of endangered or threatened species. Some of the beach areas serve as nesting sites for sea turtles, including the threatened loggerhead turtle, and the endangered green and leatherback turtles. A nesting area for the least tern, another threatened species, is set aside at the tip of Anastasia Island, within the National Monument area, just facing the Matanzas Inlet. Other species of animal life present include the endangered eastern indigo snake, the gopher frog, and the gopher tortoise. Excellent photo opportunities include possible sightings of bald eagles, ospreys, pelicans, and terns.

The Fort Matanzas National Monument is operated by the United States Park Service in conjunction with the Castillo de San Marcos National Monument and several sites in the city of St. Augustine.

History

Like the histories of Fort Caroline and Castillo de San Marcos, that of Fort Matanzas is part of the story of the struggle for control of Florida (and the North American continent) between the French and Spanish from the 1500s through the 1600s. In 1565, forces from both countries suffered great losses during the late-summer hurricane season. Attempting to reinforce the Spanish settlements at St. Augustine, King Philip II of Spain sent Pedro

Fort Matanzas has been carefully restored to match the original design. (Loretta Carlisle photo.)

French troops from Fort Caroline, shown here, were slaughtered at the site of Matanzas. (A 1591 engraving by Theodor de Bry, after a watercolor by Jacques Le Moyne. Courtesy of the Library of Congress.)

Menéndez de Avilés on a mission to destroy the budding French settlements and threats in Florida. Aviles headed an expedition of seventeen ships from Cadiz, Spain, but only two of the ships reached Puerto Rico. With three more ships he acquired there, Menéndez sailed for Florida, sighting what is now Cape Canaveral on August 28, 1565. On the same day, Jean Ribault, in command of French forces, landed five ships with reinforcements for Fort Caroline, just east of present-day Jacksonville on the St. Johns River. Menéndez sailed north, confronting the French at St. Johns River, and a few shots were fired between the two forces.

Menéndez then sailed south, and on September 8, he sailed into the inlet at the north end of Anastasia Island, where on September 8, 1565, he founded the settlement that would become St. Augustine. Learning of the Spanish settlement, Ribault embarked nearly the whole force from Fort Caroline, some five hundred men in five ships, and sailed south on September 11, despite the storm season and despite the fact that he left Fort Caroline open to land attack.

A violent storm hit the French ships, carrying them south of Anastasia Island and stranding survivors on beaches near Daytona Beach and Cape Canaveral. The survivors began the long overland march north, hoping to return to Fort Caroline by foot. As they followed the coast, they halted at the break in the shoreline at what is now Matanzas Inlet. Meanwhile, Menéndez led a force north and captured Fort Caroline, killing some 130 soldiers and civilians there, and sending some surviving women and children to captivity in Puerto Rico.

Menéndez marched some seventy Spanish troops overland southward to meet the shipwrecked French forces. Menéndez demanded their surrender, and exhausted, without weapons, and starving, the French surrendered. Using small craft, Menéndez ferried 111 of the Frenchmen across the inlet, and then the Spanish troops methodically slaughtered them, sparing only sixteen who either declared themselves Catholic or claimed to have skills as artisans that could be used in the fort construction at St. Augustine. A second group of surviving French straggled north, and the Spanish caught that group on October 11 at the same inlet. Again, the Spanish slaughtered most of the French, killing 134. A few French survivors escaped on foot to the south, where Menéndez finally caught them and sent them as prisoners to Havana. Thus there were two slaughters at the inlet, and hence the name "Matanzas" (plural, "slaughters,") not "Matanza." No archaeological evidence of the exact spot of the slaughters has ever been documented.

As the Spanish built up their fort and settlement at St. Augustine, they also built a wooden watchtower and compound at the Matanzas site, noted in 1671 by the Spanish governor in that year, Manuel de Cendoya. The Spanish always recognized that the inlet at Matanzas, and another just to the south, Penon Inlet, were vulnerable points for possible attack on St. Augustine from the sea.

During the War of Jenkins' Ear (1739–48), British forces led by Gen. James Oglethorpe attempted to take St. Augustine from

This 1743 drawing of Fort Matanzas shows idle soldiers taking potshots at passing seabirds. (Courtesy of the Library of Congress.)

the Spanish by marching overland from Georgia. The Spanish governor at the time in St. Augustine, Governor Manuel de Montiano, recognized that Spain needed a strong fort at Matanzas inlet. He intended to use a fort there to prevent an English attack from that direction, and also to keep the inlet open in case the Spanish had to evacuate the city and fort by sailing south. The obvious strategic value of the location, guarding the waterway just to the west of the tip of Anastasia Island, is still apparent.

The fort only had to be large enough to mount a few long-range guns since any ship small enough to enter through the inlets would not be able to carry heavy weapons. Furthermore, the fort would have to have high walls, which could not be easily scaled by attacking ground troops. These factors contributed to the odd, small square fortress, with one sentry box (*garita*) at one corner, the high walls, and the very limited living quarters, with a cistern for collecting and storing rainwater.

As at Castillo de San Marcos, the fort builders used coquina, quarried from nearby, but instead of the quarry near St. Augustine on Anastasia Island, they found a local source at El Penon, just south of that inlet. They covered the blocks with white lime plaster and painted the tower red. They built a projecting ridge near the top of the outside wall, designed to prevent scaling by enemy troops. The builders also painted this "scarp cordon," red. Just as at Castillo de San Marcos, the white and red color theme reflected the national colors of Spain. The scarp cordon can be seen on the reconstructed and preserved fort, as well as on models and early photos of the fort.

Later archaeological study of the fort has revealed some of the details of construction. Pine logs were driven into the ground and then capped with square pine timbers. This framework contained a footing of oyster shells. Builders raised the masonry wall on this foundation. The outside base measured a square just over 49 feet on each side at ground level. The measurement was done in Spanish "varas," a short yard of 33 inches, and the fort measured exactly 18 varas on an edge. Builders filled the center of the masonry shell with local mud. The gun deck, raised 11 feet above ground, was made of a form of concrete known as "tabby" consisting of oyster shell, sand, and crushed shells. A wooden floor built on the concrete served as the actual gun deck or floor.

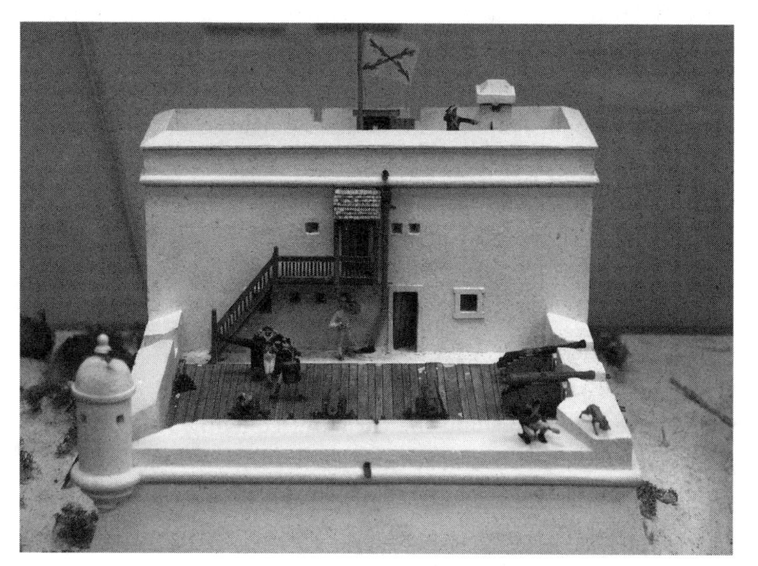

At the gift shop at Fort Matanzas, a diorama model shows the method of the fort's construction. (Loretta Carlisle photo.)

An early image of Fort Matanzas after its first restoration. (Loretta Carlisle photo of U.S. Park Service exhibit.)

Originally, a ladder provided the only entry to the fort, and it would be pulled up at night and lowered only for authorized personnel.

The armament consisted of 8-pounder cannon, and two of them from the Spanish period are still there, turned over by the Spanish when they ceded Florida to the United States in 1821. Two 6-pounder cannons are replicas, made especially for the fort for use in demonstration firings. A large, 13 × 10' brick-lined cistern under the floor of the gun deck collected rainwater, which could be removed by hoisting a bucket.

A fireplace in the soldier's quarters provided heat both for that room and for the small arched-roof officers' quarters located directly above.

Although the fort could house six guns and fifty men, through most of its history only small detachments of six or seven men would be stationed there, serving on a month's duty, then returning to St. Augustine, to be replaced by another group. Considering the size of the fort, it is hard to imagine a garrison of fifty men, unless some encamped in tents on the grounds outside the walls.

After the fort transferred to the United States, it remained unoccupied. By the early twentieth century, the walls had cracked, and large shrubs grew on the roof and gun deck. Picturesque postcards and photographs of the ruins are now collectors' items. The first effort at restoration did not come until 1916, when the U.S. Congress voted $1,025 for repairs. In 1924, President Coolidge named Fort Matanzas as a National Monument, and in 1927, the government set aside the lands around the fort and on the southern tip of Anastasia Island as a bird refuge.

The War Department transferred the partially restored ruins to the National Park Service on August 10, 1933. The National Register of Historic Places listed the fort on October 15, 1966, and added the buildings of the headquarters and visitor center to the National Register on December 31, 2008.

3 Central Florida

14

Fort Christmas

Location: Just north of SR 50 (E. Colonial Drive or Cheney Highway), near Christmas, about 20 miles east of Orlando.
Directions: From East-West Expressway/Challenger Parkway (SR 408), proceed east to exit 23 and take SR 50/520 (Colonial Drive) to the east and south, about 8.5 miles to left fork on SR 50, then east on SR 50 about 4 miles, to signs for Fort Christmas. Turn left and proceed about 1 mile north on Fort Christmas Road. The park entrance is on the left.
Hours of operation: 8 a.m. to 8 p.m., summer; 8 a.m. to 6 p.m., winter. Fort hours: 10 a.m. to 5 p.m., Tuesday through Saturday; 1 p.m. to 5 p.m., Sunday. Closed Monday and holidays. Historic homes hours: 9 a.m. to 4 p.m., Tuesday through Sunday. Closed Monday and holidays.
Fees: No admission charge for any of the facilities.
Phone: (407) 568-4149

Special Events

Organized special events at different scheduled dates throughout the year provide opportunities to meet costumed interpreters, to enjoy live performance music, or to shop for arts and crafts. It is recommended to call ahead for specific times for these events.

- Cowboy Reunion, last Saturday in January, 10 a.m. to 2 p.m.

- Militia Encampment: musket- and cannon-firing demonstrations, first weekend in April and the weekend before Thanksgiving
- Bluegrass and Craft Festival, third weekend in March
- Old Timers' Day, second Saturday in May
- Pioneer Homecoming Day, first Saturday in October
- Cracker Christmas, first weekend in December

Unique Facts

Fort Christmas got its name from the fact that, on December 25, 1837, U.S. troops and Alabama volunteers set up camp and began constructing the fort.

The structure at Fort Christmas serves as a good representation of the more than two hundred forts constructed in Florida during the Second Seminole War. This replica fort is one of the best reconstructions of any of the forts from that war, as few

The replica of a fort blockhouse at Fort Christmas is beautifully constructed; tiny windows provided excellent defensive firing positions. The second floor houses a museum with displays featuring Seminole and Florida history. (Loretta Carlisle photo.)

Adjoining Fort Christmas is a "Cracker Village," which features numerous homes transported there from the surrounding countryside and illustrating rural Florida life in the late nineteenth and early twentieth centuries. (Loretta Carlisle photo.)

traces remain of most of the forts. The original fort stood just less than one mile to the north; due to its wooden construction, the original fort has long since vanished.

Things to See

The replica fort consists of a stockaded enclosure with a single gate. One corner boasts a museum on the upper level of a log-built blockhouse (accessible by a staircase) devoted to details of the Second Seminole war. This museum display contains informative details and displays related to Osceola, the Seminoles, and especially the battles of the Second Seminole War (1835–42).

Inside the stockade, there is also a ground-level museum (wheelchair-accessible), containing displays related to rural life in Florida in the nineteenth and early twentieth centuries.

Within the compound, there is a replica of an underground powder magazine.

On the southern side of the park, about 100 yards to the south of the fort stockade, is the collection of "Historic Homes from the Cracker Era." The historic village consists of seven homes (one replica and others that have been relocated to the spot), each representing in its furnishings a slightly different period and lifestyle, showing Florida pioneer life from the 1870s through the 1950s.

The Fort Christmas Historic Park has a picnic area, a replica fort, and a collection of historic homes from the Cracker era. There is a small gift shop at the entrance to the park that is open during fort hours.

Things to See Nearby

Cape Canaveral Space Center, 27.7 miles east and south.

History

The Second Seminole War began as U.S. troops, responding to demands from new white settlers who had moved into Florida, attempted to enforce the Indian Removal Act of 1830 to remove the Seminoles from Florida and relocate them in Indian Territory, now Oklahoma. Maj. Gen Thomas S. Jesup, the overall Army commander in Florida, prepared to move the fighting to south Florida. Such preparations included road construction, with a road running on the west of the St. Johns River, crossing through difficult terrain of many creeks and wild country.

Osceola and other Seminoles and their African American allies had already fought a number of skirmishes and major battles against the advancing U.S. Army and militia troops. The advance planned by Jesup came after the Dade Battle and the killing of Indian agent Wiley Thompson by Osceola on December 28, 1835, and after several other major battles, including two defeats of the U.S. Army on the Withlacoochee River (about 39 miles west of Ocala) in 1835 and 1836. Jesup planned for several columns to converge on what he believed were the Seminole positions.

Top: This 1837 lithograph shows an encampment of troops outside a fortified house at Picolata, Florida, during the Second Seminole War. (T. F. Gray and James, Charleston, S.C., 1837. Courtesy of the Library of Congress.)

Bottom: South Carolina Dragoons inspect a ruined bridge over the Withlacoochee River during the Second Seminole War. (Lithograph issued by T. F. Gray and James, Charleston, S.C., 1837. Courtesy of the Library of Congress.)

Reenactors gather at Fort Christmas and establish authentic nineteenth-century-style campsites for their overnight stays. (Loretta Carlisle photo.)

Brig. Gen. Abraham Eustis, operating under the command of General Jesup, led a column on a march south from Fort Mellon, in what is now Sanford, Florida, starting December 17, 1837. Sanford is just to the north of Orlando, near Lake Jesup. The fort itself had originally been named Camp Monroe, but the commander of the fort, Lt. C. Alexander C. W. Fanning, named it Fort Mellon after Seminoles killed Capt. Charles Mellon in a raid. From June 14, 1837, to November 4, 1837, the fort had been abandoned. However, from 1837 through 1842, the fort acted as a supply depot and staging point. There are no remains of Fort Mellon, although Fort Mellon Park in Sanford is now a popular recreation spot.

Eustis's forces departing Fort Mellon in December 1837 included the Third Regiment of Artillery, four companies of the Third and Fourth Dragoons (cavalry troops who would march and fight dismounted as infantry), and four companies of volunteer militia from Alabama. They moved with a caravan of fifty wagons with twenty thousand rations, chopping their way through hammocks and pine woods. As the troops moved forward, they built a road, including nearly twenty bridges and seven causeways on the way to Fort Christmas.

On December 25, 1837, General Eustis had his troops set up camp on the north side of Christmas Creek, less than a mile from the present Fort Christmas site. They constructed a depot made from pine logs, with two 20-foot-high square blockhouses at opposite corners.

As they pushed south, the Army established several more posts to serve as depots for movement of troops and supplies further on in their route. Fort Gatlin, Fort Maitland, Fort Christmas, and Fort McNeil were all built within what is now Orange County. Two other "Fort Gatlins" existed at one time or another in Florida, but this particular Fort Gatlin was located on Lake Gatlin, just a couple of miles directly south of modern downtown Orlando. Fort Gatlin Recreational Park at the site now contains a swimming facility and tennis courts at 2009 Lake Margaret Drive. The fort (and the later park) got its name from Dr. John Gatlin, killed in the Dade Battle on December 28, 1835. Fort Maitland, located near the center of what is now Maitland, was named for Capt. William Seton Maitland, who was wounded in the Battle of Wahoo Swamp on November 21, 1836. Fort McNeil was located just a few miles southeast of Fort Christmas near the shore of the St. Johns River in what is today Tosohatchee State Game Preserve. That fort was named for 2nd Lt. John Winfield Scott McNeil, nephew of President Franklin Pierce. McNeil died in battle with Native Americans near Dunlawton on January 17, 1836. None of these Orange County forts had any battles directly on their site. A historical marker in Maitland identifies the site of Fort Maitland, and only Fort Christmas now stands as a representation of this phase of the Second Seminole War, as the others either burned down or simply vanished as the wooden construction rotted out. In fact, Fort Christmas, as a reconstructed blockhouse, along with Fort Foster, are two of the best places to visit for visualizing conditions faced by U.S. troops during the Second Seminole War.

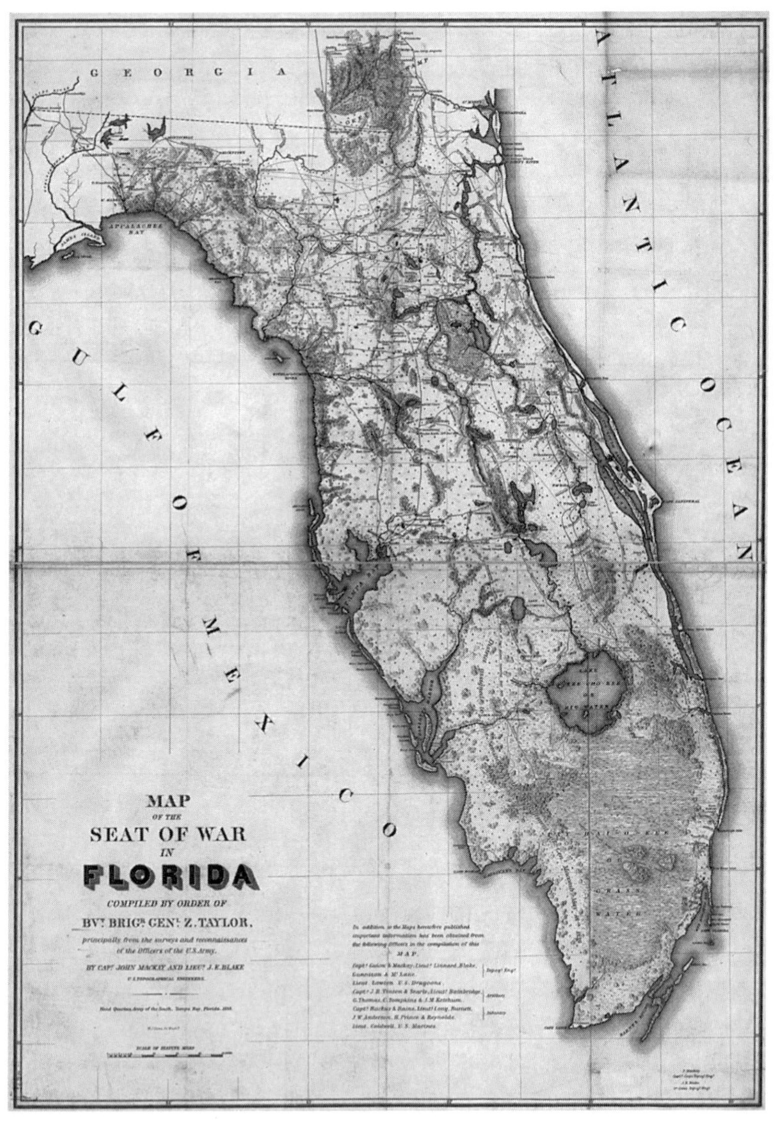

This *Map of the Seat of War in Florida* was compiled in 1839 by order of General Zachary Taylor. (Loretta Carlisle photo of display at Fort Foster.)

The Simmons house at the Cracker Village at Fort Christmas was originally built about 1915 by George Simmons near Taylor Creek, not far from Fort Christmas. The construction is a fine example of the style, with a wide porch, a central living room, end bedrooms, and a separate kitchen. (Loretta Carlisle photo.)

After the troops set up Fort Christmas, General Eustis led a column south in early January 1838. He left Major Mann Page Lomax in charge of two companies of artillery as a garrison at the fort as he advanced. He moved south under orders from Jesup to be part of a pincers movement against the Seminoles, which did not succeed. Soon, the advancing troops could receive supplies by water route from the St. Lucie River and Jupiter Inlet on the Atlantic coast, and by March 1838, the troops abandoned Fort Christmas. The Alabama troops returned north to Fort Mellon, then went home. The 80 × 80' pine-log fort soon fell into disrepair and rotted away, but it gave its name to the nearby town of Christmas.

The Orange County Parks and Recreation Commission built the present replica fort, starting in the bicentennial year of 1976, (dedicated on December 17, 1977), and the fort is maintained by the county commission with the help of volunteers organized in the Fort Christmas Historical Society.

The Cracker Village

The replica and moved Cracker houses are well worth a visit, as they show living conditions, furnishings, day-to-day work, and other aspects of pioneer nineteenth- and early-twentieth-century life in Florida. They include a replica of a mid-nineteenth-century Florida pioneer home with a sugarcane grinder, a stand of sugarcane, and an orange grove. Just to the south and west of the main house are the houses of pioneers Wheeler and Annie Bass (built in about 1905), Dixie and Emma Partin (about 1950), the Simmons family (1880s), the Yates family (1890s), the Brown family, the Woods family, and a house from the Bee Head Ranch dating to about 1915. The homes and grounds also have displays regarding early Florida life including such products as sugarcane, citrus fruit, and turpentine, as well as early cattle raising. The term "Cracker" is thought to derive from the long cattle whips that would be cracked over the heads of cattle when driving them from place to place or flushing them out of marshes and woods. The term was also used in a pejorative way to refer to Scots-Irish (or "Borderlands" English) settlers in the southern backwoods.

15

Dade Battlefield

Location: Off I-75 at Bushnell exit.
Driving Directions: From I-75, take the Bushnell exit 314 and head east on CR 48. Watch for the signs off to the right at about 1 mile, then proceed about one mile south on CR 603 to the park entrance.
Hours of Operation: The visitor center is open from 9 a.m. to 5 p.m., Thursday through Monday. Closed Tuesday and Wednesday. The park grounds are open dawn to dusk, 365 days a year.
Fees: $3 per vehicle paid by envelope drop.
Phone: (352) 793-4781

Special Events

A reenactment of the battle is usually scheduled for the first Sunday in January every year. Call ahead to confirm date and time.

Other special events are scheduled from time to time, such as a Tin Can Camper Rally later in January, a World War II Day in August, and other events such as a Seminole swap meet. For dates and upcoming events, visitors should call ahead.

Unique Facts

The battle that took place on December 28, 1835, became the major event precipitating the Second Seminole War, which lasted from 1835 to 1842.

Entrance to the Dade Battlefield, a few miles east of I-75 in central Florida. (Loretta Carlisle photo.)

Things to See

The park and visitor center are located at the spot where the battle took place. Across from the visitor center, a small, low, log structure represents the hastily erected defensive position of the surrounded U.S. troops.

Although no visible evidence of the battle can be seen, the visitor center has an excellent display giving a full account of the battle and exhibiting a collection of contemporary and replica weapons and artifacts from the period. Dioramas depict the tactics of the Seminoles as they attacked the marching column of U.S. troops.

Park staff are knowledgeable about the history of the event and willingly answer questions. A twelve-minute video entitled *This Land, These Men* gives a balanced account of the battle.

Things to See Nearby

The park and surrounding countryside have open fields with scattered pine trees, native grasses, and clumps of palmettos. A half-mile nature trail winds through pine flat woods, where a visitor might spy gopher tortoises, songbirds, woodpeckers, hawks, cranes, and indigo snakes.

The nearest sites of military history interest are Fort Foster in Hillsborough River State Park (about 41 miles to the south) and Fort Cooper (about 20 miles to the northwest).

History

In 1835, it became obvious to the U.S. Army, white settlers, and the state government of Florida that large numbers of Seminoles were unwilling to be relocated to the Indian Territory (now Oklahoma). Some leaders had accepted payment to remove to the West, but many others thought those who did were traitors or sell-outs. Although the government planned to bring in bands of Seminoles, take them to Fort Brooke in Tampa, and to transport them from there to New Orleans for a river trip up to Arkansas

At the site of the Dade Battlefield, this small assemblage of logs represents the hastily erected defensive position of the U.S. troops who were nearly all killed there in 1835, an event which set off the Second Seminole War. (Loretta Carlisle photo.)

Tustennuggee Emathla, shown here, was a Creek chief who sided with U.S. Army troops against the Seminoles in the Second Seminole War. (McKenney & Hall lithograph print, ca. 1838. Courtesy of the Library of Congress.)

and an overland trip to the Indian Territory, only some Seminoles trusted the promises of the government.

Promises had been made and broken before, and the Seminoles and their African American allies simply wanted to be left alone to live in peace in Florida. Furthermore, the government refused to pledge that the African Americans among the Seminoles would not be sold back into slavery.

Not only were many Seminoles and African Americans among them unwilling to be relocated, but some were prepared to resist relocation by force of arms. Throughout the white settlements, Florida began preparing for war. In St. Augustine, the local militia asked the government for five hundred muskets and began drilling volunteers. Osceola led a war party that seized militia supply wagons. Sugar plantations near St. Augustine were attacked, and some of the slaves from the plantations escaped to join the Seminoles.

The ill-prepared U.S. Army could not quickly deal with the threat. The small army, scattered across the frontier, had to maintain peace in the Indian Territory and guard both the Canadian border and many seacoast forts. European American settlers in Florida demanded protection.

Altogether, eleven companies of regular U.S. troops quartered in Florida, numbering something more than five hundred troops. Fort King, just to the east of present-day Ocala, had one company of troops, and authorities feared that that small contingent (about fifty troops) would be easily overrun by the Seminoles. Although the Army had no clear count of Seminole warriors, rumors suggested they numbered in the thousands. Even a more realistic estimate of a small group of a few hundred represented a formidable threat to the Fort King outpost because the Seminoles understood exactly how to conduct what is now called "unconventional warfare," using ambushes and night attacks and not attempting to hold fortified positions.

Three more companies of U.S. troops were stationed at Fort Brooke in Tampa, and two more were due to arrive there by

This 1837 lithograph of U.S. troops fording the Oklawaha River during the Second Seminole War raises the obvious question: Why didn't they use the bridge? (T. F. Gray and James, Charleston, S.C., 1837. Courtesy of the Library of Congress.)

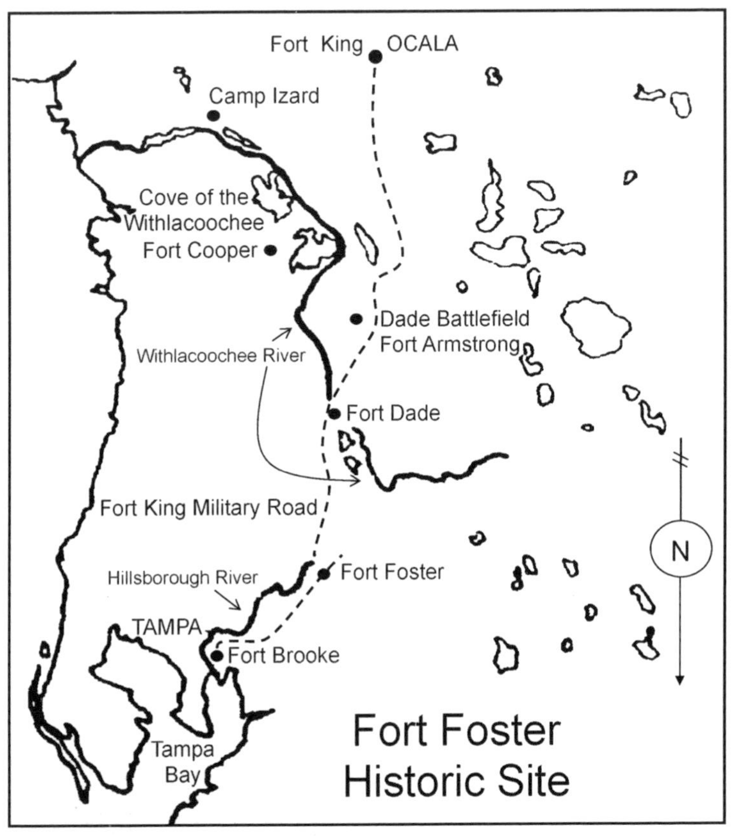

This map provided at Fort Foster shows the 1830s route from Fort Brooke (Tampa) to Fort King (Ocala). (Florida Park Service.)

ship. The actual site of Fort Brooke can no longer be visited, as it vanished long ago, and the modern Tampa Convention Center is built over the location of the fort. The Army decided to reinforce Fort King by marching two companies overland from Fort Brooke to Fort King, along a major route. That north-south military road is roughly the line now followed by US 301 in this part of the state.

The two companies, about 110 men, marched out of Fort Brooke on December 23, under the command of Maj. Francis L. Dade, who rode horseback at the head of the column.

Seminole warriors under the leadership of Micanopy and Jumper scouted the marching column. The U.S. troops, burdened with heavy blue wool coats, plodded northward, making about 10 to 15 miles a day. Many wore their heavy overcoats against the chill, draped over their weapons. On December 28, the Seminoles ambushed the troops, firing at them from behind cover of trees and palmettos. Maj. Francis Dade died first, and the troops struggled to get their heavy woolen coats off and to load and fire their muskets. Most were quickly shot down as the Seminole forces fired from their left and front. A small group of the soldiers hastily arranged a log barrier from which to return fire. In addition to muskets, they had a small cannon (from which one cannonball has been retrieved from a nearby farm in recent years). But the last group of soldiers behind the logs soon ran out of ammunition, and the attackers slaughtered them as well. Only three of the 110 survived, and one was killed the next day, making it one of the deadliest Indian attacks in U.S. history. Two survivors, Ransome Clarke and Joseph Sprague, both wounded and exhausted, walked back to Fort Brooke. Sprague had hidden in a pond so he had not witnessed the battle and could not give an account of it, but Clarke submitted a report.

When troops arrived after the battle, they were shocked to find the scattered skeletons of the soldiers. ("Massacre of Major Dade and his Command," 1847 engraving from Barber's *Incidents in American History*. Loretta Carlisle photo of Dade Battlefield Park Exhibit.)

The Second Seminole War saw atrocities on both sides. Gen. Abraham Eustis ordered the burning of the African Seminole town of Pilak-li-ka-ha. (Lithograph issued by T. F. Gray and James, Charleston, S.C., 1837. Courtesy of the Library of Congress.)

The tactics of the attacking band of Seminoles were classic ambush, and brilliantly carried out. They lost only three men and five wounded out of their force of some 180 Seminole and black warriors. The Second Seminole War had begun with this attack and with a much smaller ambush the same day near Fort King, in which Osceola and his troops killed Wiley Thompson and six others.

At Fort Brooke, the news of the defeat came as a shock. Maj. Ethan Allen Hitchcock, in the expedition that arrived at the scene of the battle in February, reported his dismay at the sight of the bodies, now reduced to skeletons, scattered where they had fallen.

However, Hitchcock privately blamed government policy for arousing what he called the "persevering opposition of the Indians, who have nobly defended their country against our attempt to enforce a fraudulent treaty." Over the next seven years, the United States would fight its most expensive war (in terms of the value of current dollars and lives lost) prior to the Civil War. The expenditures during the Second Seminole war came to some $30 million.

16

Fort Cooper

Location: Just off US 41, on South Old Floral City Road, two miles south of the center of Inverness.
Driving Directions: From Inverness, proceed south on US 41, about two miles and turn left on South Old City Road; watch for entrance to the Fort Cooper Park on the right.
Hours of Operation: 8 a.m. until sundown, 365 days a year.
Fees: $2 per vehicle (limit 8 people per vehicle). $1 per person for pedestrians, bicyclists, extra passengers, passengers in vehicles with a holder of an Annual Individual Entrance Pass. Primitive tent camping fee, $4 per person per day (reservations required). Organized youth and adult group camping, $1 per youth, $2 per adult/chaperone.
Phone: (352) 726-0315

Special Events

An excellent reenactment of skirmishes of the Second Seminole War is conducted annually on the third weekend in March. The reenactment represents a short siege and several shootouts that took place in 1836. Reenactors include representatives of the Georgia militia volunteers, the U.S. Army, the Seminole Indians, and horse-mounted African American freedom fighters who fought as allies of the Seminoles.

The reenactors set up encampments at the site. Those representing the U.S. and Georgia forces pitch their tents directly at the fort site, while those representing the Seminoles and their

Reenactors in both Seminole and militia outfits fire muskets in this skirmish at Fort Cooper. The reenactment is usually scheduled for the third weekend in March each year. (Loretta Carlisle photo.)

African American allies camp nearby in a clearing in the woods. Authentic camp life of the 1830s is represented with clothing, artifacts, tents, fire pits, handicrafts, cooking, and weaponry. During the reenactment weekend, several vendors of handicrafts and publications sell their wares at outside retail stalls.

Unique Facts

The "fort" was not really a fort. U.S. troops and Georgia militia volunteers began erecting a stockade in 1836, but never completed it. The fort or military encampment site is about a half-mile walk from the main park picnic area, down a trail that runs alongside Lake Holathlikaha (also known as Fort Cooper Lake). During special events, a tractor-pulled shuttle takes passengers to the fort site.

Things to See

The partially completed stockade wall, made of standing logs, is all that represents the actual fortification. Visitors who tour the site on days when there is no reenactment have to use their imagination to visualize the siege of the U.S. Army troops and the Georgia militia volunteers by the encircling Seminole and African Seminole warriors.

Swimming and fishing are allowed in the lake, depending on the water level.

Things to See Nearby

Homosassa Springs State Wildlife Park, 19.4 miles west.

Coastal Heritage Museum, 532 Citrus Ave., Crystal River, 18.5 miles west.

Dade Battlefield, 19.4 miles southeast. The battle there in December 1835 marked the beginning of the Second Seminole War.

Fort Foster, 46.8 miles southeast.

This replica stockade is the only structure at Fort Cooper representing the temporary fort built there in 1836, during the Second Seminole War. (Loretta Carlisle photo.)

History

There were three Seminole Wars in Florida:

- First Seminole War 1817–18
- Second Seminole War 1835–42
- Third Seminole War 1855–58 (also known as Billy Bowlegs' War)

The First Seminole War ran its course before Florida became a territory of the United States. U.S. forces, commanded by Andrew Jackson, invaded Spanish-held West Florida in pursuit of fugitive slaves and African American settlers living among the Seminoles. Seminoles and their African American allies had established well-stocked and armed forts and settlements in what is now Northwest Florida. The history of those events is related in the entries in this guidebook for Fort Gadsden and Fort San Marcos de Apalache. The presence of armed groups and those of white traders who helped provide them with weapons served as constant irritations to slaveholding planters in Georgia and Alabama. With an eye to expansion into Florida, U.S. authorities sanctioned Jackson's expedition. After several defeats, and Jackson's execution of British agents engaged in supplying arms to the Indians and the African American allies, the Seminoles and their black allies simply retreated southward to the interior.

After the acquisition of Florida by the United States in 1821, white settlers from Georgia began to seek out the best lands and to establish farms and ranches, taking over hunting grounds and cattle-grazing territory used by the Seminoles. After a series of clashes, the Seminoles and U.S. authorities signed a treaty. Under the Treaty of Paynes Landing (1832), the Seminoles were supposed to migrate west of the Mississippi River within three years. The U.S. authorities disagreed about whether the African Americans living among the Seminoles could migrate west as free people, or whether they should be reenslaved. The wording of the Treaty of Paynes Landing left unclear whether the three-year period began in 1832 or with the first shipment west.

By 1834, the U.S. government had forcibly moved more than 3,800 Seminoles by ship, riverboat, and overland trails to settlements in what is now Oklahoma. However, a large faction of Seminoles resisted, under the leadership of Osceola, and they refused to leave. On December 28, 1835, Osceola killed Indian agent Wiley Thompson. On the same day, a group of about three hundred Seminole and African American fighters ambushed Maj. Francis Dade and his two companies of U.S. troops as they marched north from Fort Brooke (in Tampa) toward Fort King. Fort King no longer exists, but it stood just to the east of present-day Ocala. These two incidents began the Second Seminole War. Despite numerous engagements, the Seminoles retreated into forested and swampy areas to the south. There were hundreds of casualties on both sides as the war continued over the next seven years.

By 1837, the Seminoles had succeeded enough in their resistance that the U.S. forces agreed to discuss a truce. During negotiations, however, General Jesup treacherously had Osceola arrested and confined, first at Castillo de San Marcos (then known as Fort Marion) in Saint Augustine, and then later at Fort Moultrie at Charleston, South Carolina. Osceola died there on January 30, 1838. His followers continued the struggle. By 1842, exhausted and constantly driven from their sources of food, with their cattle stolen, most of them agreed to a peace settlement but not an official treaty.

At the end of the Second Seminole war in 1842, about 4,400 Seminoles surrendered and accepted transportation to the Indian Territory (Oklahoma), accompanied by many of the Afro-Seminole people. Several hundred Seminoles remained in the Everglades, followers of Billy Bowlegs, their principal leader. He led an uprising in the late 1850s known as the Third Seminole War. Although U.S. forces declared that war completed in 1858, it simply ended without a treaty and with the Seminoles remaining in the Everglades; their descendants took the position that the Seminoles had never surrendered to the United States.

The Second Seminole War, with its siege and skirmishes at Fort Cooper, became the most expensive of the Indian Wars for

Chief Tuko See Mathla supported the U.S. government's plan to move the Seminoles to Oklahoma. (McKenney & Hall lithograph print, ca. 1843. Courtesy of the Library of Congress.)

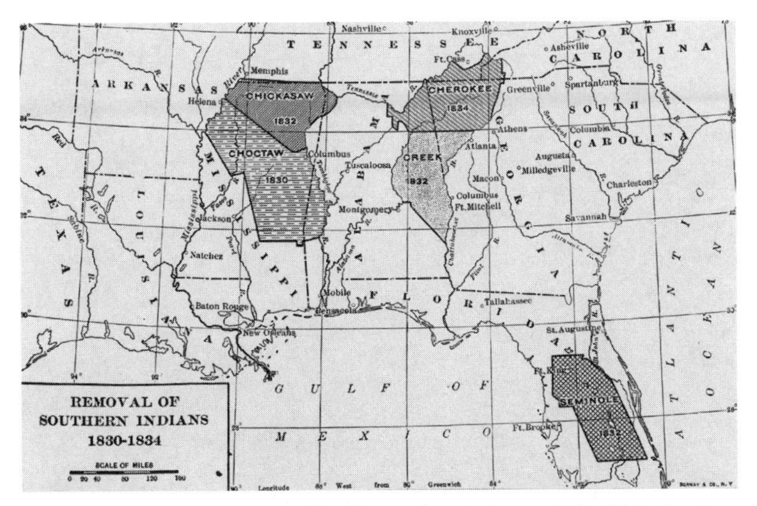

Dixon Ryan Fox's map, *Removal of the Southern Indians, 1830–1834*, identifies the Native American nations subjected to forced relocation. (From *Atlas of American History*, Harper and Brothers, 1920).

the United States in the pre–Civil War era. It cost the lives of thousands of Seminoles and their black allies and an estimated 1,500 U.S. soldiers. The dollar cost exceeded $30 million (an amount that would be equivalent to several billion dollars today).

Fort Cooper in the Second Seminole War

The encampment spot was later called Fort Cooper in memory of Maj. Mark Anthony Cooper. Cooper commanded five companies of the First Georgia Battalion of Volunteers. In April 1836, Cooper stayed behind with wounded and sick troops at Lake Holathlikaha. They made camp near the lake's water supply. Meanwhile, other troops, under the command of Gen. Winfield Scott, headed south toward what is now Tampa in pursuit of a large band of Seminoles.

For sixteen days, Cooper and his troops defended the small outpost, sustaining a siege by both Seminoles and African American freedom fighters. The lake provided drinking water for both the men and some cattle they had brought along as a living meat supply. In several raids, the Seminoles and African American

The Georgia Militia took up a defensive position at Fort Cooper, near Lake Holathlikaha, where they held off a Seminole siege that lasted more than two weeks. (Loretta Carlisle photo.)

The besieged militia and U.S. army troops at Fort Cooper used a small field cannon similar to this one, on display during the annual reenactment. (Loretta Carlisle photo.)

fighters ran off the cattle. In an early form of psychological warfare, the attackers then barbecued beefsteaks in the woods nearby; the Georgia Volunteers, facing starvation as their rations dwindled, were tantalized by the smoke from the roasting beefsteaks. On April 18, Scott returned to the little encampment, bringing supplies and reinforcements for the approximately 380 troops at the camp. The reenactment held annually on the third weekend of March represents this siege. After the reenacted skirmish, the reenactors step out of their 1836 roles to give brief lectures describing the events and the historical context.

Private owners sold 710 acres in several lots in 1970 to establish the park. After installation of trails, picnic areas, and parking lots, Fort Cooper opened to the public as a Florida State Park in 1977.

17

Fort Chokonikla/ Paynes Creek

Location: South of Fort Meade and Bowling Green on US 17.
Driving Directions: From I-75, take exit 257 to SR 60 East to Bartow, and turn right (south on US 17), passing through Fort Meade and Bowling Green. Follow US 17 to Bowling Green, and then follow the signs at Main Street east to Lake Branch Road, then to the Paynes Creek Historic State Park.
Hours of Operation: Park: 8 a.m. until sunset daily. Visitor center: 9 a.m. to 5 p.m. daily.
Fees: No admission charge.
Phone: (863) 375-4717

Unique Facts

Fort Chokonikla served as the first of a line of forts built in 1849 after the Second Seminole War in order to separate the Seminole reservation country to the south from white settlements to the north. The fort never suffered an attack, but the Army abandoned it less than a year after building it.

Things to See

Although there are no visible remains of the fort, the visitor center maintains an excellent exhibit explaining the purpose of the fort. By following a marked trail through the woods and across a

The visitor center at Paynes Creek State Park has extensive information about Fort Chokonikla. (Loretta Carlisle photo.)

footbridge, visitors can locate a fenced-in monument that commemorates the destruction of the Kennedy-Darling Trading Post by renegade Seminoles in 1849.

Hiking trails, picnic pavilions, and canoe and kayak launch points make the Paynes Creek Park an attraction for fishing, boating, birding, hiking, and botanical exploration. A youth camping area provides a site for primitive camping. The Peace River and Paynes Creek provide good fishing grounds for bream, catfish, bass, and snook.

At the visitor center, a historical video is shown on weekends and holidays at 11 a.m., 1 p.m., and 3 p.m.

Things to See Nearby

The Paynes Creek State Park that contains the site of Fort Chokonikla is relatively remote from other sites of military interest. However, an extended day trip might include other Seminole War–period locations including the Dade Battlefield (about 85 miles north) and Hillsborough State Park, which includes Fort Foster (about 50 miles north).

A hike through the woods takes the visitor to this small memorial commemorating the death of two traders, part of the cause of Billy Bowlegs' War (Third Seminole War) in the 1850s. (Loretta Carlisle photo.)

History

The Second Seminole War lasted from 1835 to 1842, and resulted in an uneasy peace between the Seminole people, the advancing tide of white settlement, and the U.S. government. While some Seminole leaders had agreed, under certain conditions, to accept emigration to what is now Oklahoma, large numbers of Seminoles refused to be deported. They had retreated into a largely unmapped and unexplored (by whites) territory south and east of Tampa, Florida. Federal authorities attempted to establish a trading post on the northern edge of this ill-defined reservation, known as the Kennedy-Darling Store or Trading Post, in 1849.

No sooner did the small post open than a band of Seminoles attacked and destroyed it, killing the traders George Payne and Dempsey Whidden. A survivor, William McCullough, fled with his wife and child into the woods. In reaction, the Army began work on a chain of forts across Florida, and Fort Chokonikla, a half mile from the site of the trading post on high ground, the first of the chain, opened in October 1849.

The isolation of the post and infestation by malaria-carrying mosquitoes led to the abandonment of the fort within a year. The fifteen other hastily built forts in the chain served for a few years as a barrier and a means of confining the Seminoles south of a line that ran in an arc across the state and down the Atlantic coast.

Although only a few historic markers and town place-names now mark that chain of forts, the line can be traced on modern maps by noting the location of several towns later built at the fort locations. These include small towns and large cities, running in a line from west to east and down the Atlantic coast: Fort Green, Fort Meade, Fort Kissimmee, Fort Drum, Fort Pierce, and Fort Lauderdale. Fort Hamer Road in Parrish, Florida, and Fort Crawford Creek in Manatee County mark other locations. An

At Fort Chokonikla, this display of the Darling Store inside the museum shows the sorts of trade goods and supplies sold in the 1850s. (Loretta Carlisle photo.)

During the Second and Third Seminole Wars, stockaded Army forts like this one withstood attacks. (Lithograph issued by T. F. Gray and James, Charleston, S.C., 1837. Courtesy of the Library of Congress.)

Neamathla, shown here, was opposed to removal of the Seminoles from Florida, and Governor William P. Duval ordered him "deposed" from his position as chief. (McKenney & Hall lithograph print, n.d. Courtesy of the Library of Congress.)

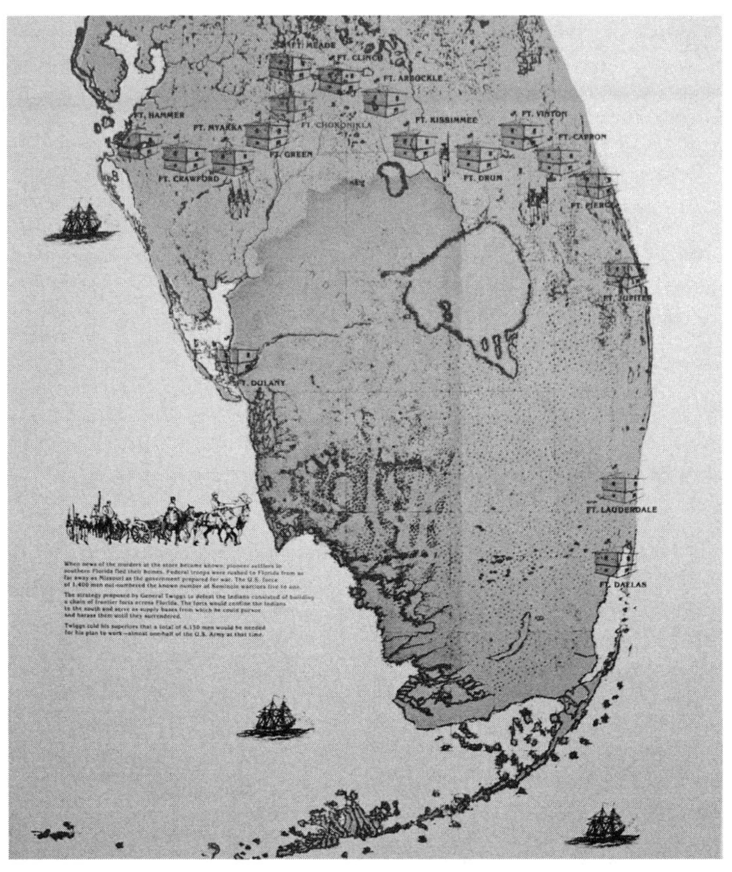

This wall display at the Paynes Creek State Park visitor center shows the chain of forts that once ran across Florida from Fort Hammer (or Hamer) on the Gulf coast to Jupiter and down to Fort Lauderdale and Fort Dallas (Miami) on the Atlantic coast. (Loretta Carlisle photo.)

excellent display map in the visitor center shows the location of these forts as well as the others that do not survive in modern place-names.

The visitor center also shows the layout and method of construction of these wooden forts. A work party of about one hundred men would clear the trees in an area of a few acres to establish clear fields of fire from the fort. A square palisade wall would be built, often with one or more blockhouses at the corners. Excavations at the Fort Chokonikla site have not turned up the remains of a wall at this location, and experts conclude that there may not have been an outer wall at this short-lived fort. Today all that remains of the fort site at Fort Chokonikla is a cleared sandy area marked by tortoise and bird tracks.

The construction of the chain of forts and encroaching settlement led to what has been called the Third Seminole War, which started December 20, 1855, and lasted for about two and a half years. Following Seminole leader Billy Bowlegs, remnants of his small force finally surrendered in May 1858, consisting of thirty-eight warriors and eighty-five women and children. As noted in other entries, not all Seminoles agreed to the surrender, and descendants later took pride in the fact that they belonged to a nation of Native Americans that had never surrendered to the U.S. government.

Over the years following the Third Seminole War, the Army abandoned almost all of the forts, and the structures fell into disrepair. Some burned down, either accidentally, or as victims of arson or vandalism. It is quite possible that the troops themselves started at least some of the fires as a way of ending what must have seemed horrible duty, with heat, mosquitoes, snakes, and the endless tedium of fort life. In some cases, like that of Fort Hamer, the Army sold the materials or removed them to construct other forts. Today the chain of forts across the state that left so many place-names is almost entirely forgotten and the forts are vanished, best commemorated in the visitor center of Fort Chokonikla.

At the Paynes Creek State Park, a long walk through the woods on "Historic Trail No. 2" leads to the bridge crossing Paynes Creek to a small monument noting the death of the traders at the store. Farther along the trail, from an overview location, a small structure representing the original location of the trading post can be seen in the woods across the creek.

In 1978, the National Register of Historic Places listed the site of Fort Chokonikla. The state took title to the land containing the monument to the traders who had been killed at the trading post. The state extended the park to some 410 acres, and opened it to the public in 1981.

18

Fort Foster

Location: The replica fort and bridge are located in Hillsborough State Park, on US 301, 6 miles south of Zephyrhills. The historic site is on the east side of the highway, but is entered by way of the main park entrance on the west side of US 301.
Driving Directions: *From the north on I-75*, take exit 279 to SR 54 east to Zephyrhills; turn right (south) on US 301 and drive 6 miles to the park entrance. *From the south on I-75*, take exit 285, proceed east on SR 582 to US 301, then north about 9 miles to the park entrance.
Hours of Operation: Fort Foster is not open for visitation on a daily basis and does not have regular operating hours. The fort is opened for guided tours and for special events.
Fees: $4 per vehicle (limit 8 people per vehicle). $3 for single occupant in a vehicle. $3 for pedestrians, bicyclists, extra passengers, passengers in vehicles with holder of Annual Individual Entrance Pass. $1 per person for members of organized groups.
Tour Times: 2 p.m., Thursday and Saturday; 11 a.m., Sunday (no tour on Monday, Tuesday, Wednesday, and Friday). Visitors join the tour at the interpretative center in Hillsborough State Park, and a towed trolley takes them across US 301 to the site. Closed Monday, Tuesday, Wednesday, and Friday.
Phone: (813) 987-6771

Fort Foster is a careful replica of a Second Seminole War–era fort, with a stockade surrounding a large inner court and a blockhouse at the corner. Wall slits allowed firing down on any attackers. (Loretta Carlisle photo.)

Special Events

Reenactors schedule displays and skirmishes at the park in February and provide interpretive information on the history of the fort and the period. Call ahead for scheduled dates and times.

Unique Facts

The replica fort and replica bridge have been built with great historical accuracy and represent one of the best sites in Florida for visualizing fort conditions during the Second Seminole War period.

Things to See

The park provides pavilions and picnic facilities for groups. Seven pavilions (Sabal, Cypress, Palmetto, Miccosukee, Smokehouse, Gator, and Blazing Star) are available for reservation.

A recreational hall is equipped with a kitchen and is also available for reservation with or without the use of the kitchen. The "Spirit of the Woods" poolside cafe and gift shop offers breakfast and lunch menus. The gift shop carries camp necessities, souvenirs, field guides, and books related to the park and to Florida. Canoe and bike rentals are available at the shop. Hikers enjoy well-marked trails to bridges over the Hillsborough River and throughout the larger park areas.

During the days the fort is open and when reenactors are present, visitors can learn details of fort life, observe the methods of construction, including the placement of loopholes in the outer stockade walls, and walk across the reconstructed bridge over the Hillsborough River. Living quarters, artifacts, powder magazine, stockade walls, gate, and arrangement of armaments all give authentic views of how such forts were maintained during the Second Seminole War, 1835–42.

A close look at the interpretive center near the highway is rewarding as it reflects the style and method employed by the

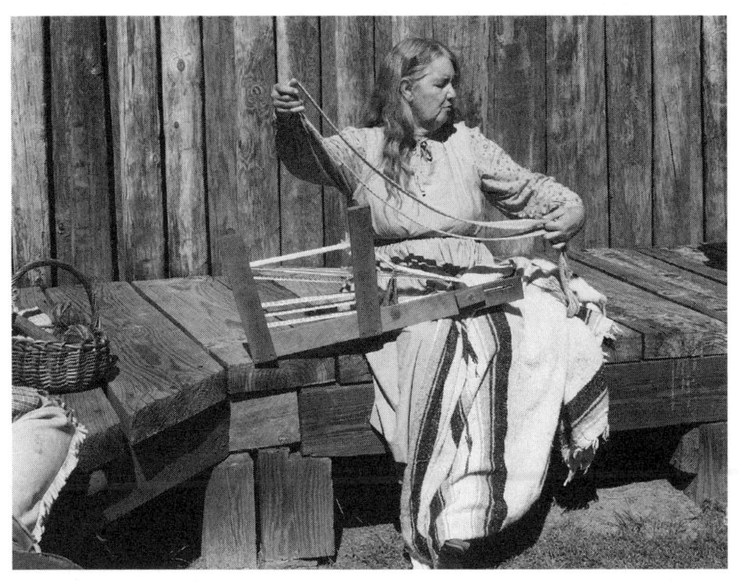

Life for soldiers' and officers' wives at Fort Foster involved the practice of domestic handicrafts, as demonstrated by this reenactor with a lap loom. (Loretta Carlisle photo.)

Civilian Conservation Corps (CCC) in their construction of park facilities in the 1930s. This interpretive center is open even on days the fort itself is closed.

On display in the interpretive center are a number of artifacts recovered during archaeological work, such as small cannonballs from the swivel guns mounted in the fort, flintlock musket parts, sheets of lead used for making musket flint patches, musket flints, leather shoe soles, iron mule shoes, buckles, a jackknife, and fishhooks. Other displays and illustrations in the center explain how the Seminole military tactics of using the natural environment, planning ambushes, adapting Western weapons, and massing superior numbers at key transit points frustrated the U.S. government's attempts to subdue them and deport them to Oklahoma.

This lithograph print published around 1848 depicts Zachary Taylor, as commander of U.S. forces, hunting down Seminoles with dogs, a practice that outraged the North. (Published by James Baillie, New York, N.Y. Courtesy of the Library of Congress.)

Demonstrating scenes of daily life among the Seminoles, two reenactors pose as a warrior and his "captive wife." They are shown here standing on the reconstructed bridge near the fort. (Loretta Carlisle photo.)

Things to See Nearby

Fort Foster is about 39 miles south of the Dade Battlefield (by following US 301), where the Second Seminole War began in December 1835. By way of I-75, the distance is 55 miles.

Fort De Soto, south of St. Petersburg, is 47 miles by way of I-4.

History

Fort Foster was built as Fort Alabama on the military road that connected Fort Brooke (in present-day Tampa) to Fort King (just east of present-day Ocala). At the crossing of the Hillsborough River, Seminoles set up ambush points and destroyed temporary bridges there several times. As a consequence, the Army built the fort in March 1836. Alabama volunteers booby-trapped the original fort, blowing it up. Fort Foster was built later in 1836 to replace the original fort, with troops and light artillery protecting the bridge from further attack.

Powder magazines in log forts like this one at Fort Foster were often built partly underground and isolated from the outer walls of the fort so that accidental detonations would be less likely. (Loretta Carlisle photo.)

In 1836, Col. William S. Foster left the fort with the bulk of the troops, leaving Navy Lt. L. Leib in command of about fifty seamen, and some twenty men of the Third and Fourth U.S. Army Artillery regiments. Together with some militia volunteers encamped outside the fort, they were to protect the fort and to staff it. On January 20, 1837, the Seminole forces fired on the militia volunteer group encamped nearby. A runner went to Fort Brooke to ask for reinforcements, and 150 marines were soon dispatched, tripling the force at the garrison.

On February 3, 1837, the Seminoles attacked again in an attempt to burn the bridge, but were repulsed. This engagement was the last battle of the Second Seminole War fought at this fort. Troops abandoned the fort in 1838 because the site became so unhealthy. The Army briefly reactivated the fort in 1849 when authorities believed the Seminoles would rise again.

The Civilian Conservation Corps (CCC) built the park in 1936, and it became the first park in the Florida State Park system. The present-day interpretive center now occupies the original

CCC-built entrance gatehouse for the park. The interpretive center contains displays of historical information about the original fort as well as about the CCC construction effort.

A local rancher deeded the site of the fort itself to the Florida State Park system in 1973. After detailed historical and archaeological research, the State Division of Recreation and Parks reconstructed the present-day replica of Fort Foster and the bridge it protected on almost exactly the original site. The fort is slightly offset so that construction of the replica did not disturb valuable yet-undiscovered archaeological evidence.

19

Fort De Soto

Location: On Mullet Key, south of St. Petersburg. Address: 3500 Pinellas Bayway South.
Driving Directions. From I-275 in St. Petersburg, take exit 17 West to SR 682, Pinellas Bayway. Proceed to Isla del Sol, and turn left on CR 679 (Pinellas Bayway South) (toll). Continue south to Fort De Soto Park and to Anderson Boulevard (tall flagpole). Turn right and follow Anderson Boulevard to the end and the park parking lot.
Hours of Operation: Park: 8 a.m. to 5 p.m. daily. Campground office: 8 a.m. to 9 p.m., Friday and Saturday; 8 a.m. to 6 p.m., Sunday through Thursday.
Fees: There is no admission charge to the fort grounds or the Quartermaster Museum, although there is a small toll on the access road. For overnight camping, there is a per-night fee that varies with the site selected. For current fees and reservations, check the Pinellas County website shown below.
Phone: Park office: (727) 893-9185. Campground office: (727) 893-9185. Automated information message: (727) 582-2267.
Website: www.pinellascounty.org/park

Unique Facts

In addition to its historic fort, Fort De Soto Park, maintained by the Pinellas County Park Department, is the location of one of the best beaches in the United States. In fact, it has been ranked by several beach experts as *the* best beach in the United States.

The park has a section of beach on which dogs are allowed, making it the only dog-friendly beach in Florida.

Fort De Soto Park is the largest park in the Pinellas County Park system. Fort De Soto is one of very few coastal defense facilities built specifically in response to the Spanish-American War (1898). Fort De Soto Park covers 1,136 acres over five interconnected islands. The remaining 12-inch mortars on display are the only ones of the type still in existence in the United States. The only others in the world are on Corregidor Island in the Philippines.

Things to See

The concealed gun emplacements, behind high concrete and sand-banked walls, together with the now-empty magazines and fire-control rooms, give a clear picture of how this early-twentieth-century coastal fortification worked. A nearby small museum across the parking lot from the fortifications provides a

This 12-inch, 1890-vintage mortar, in a concealed emplacement behind the sand dunes, was turned by hand cranks to a firing position; the shells had a 6.8-mile range, protecting the entrance to Tampa Bay. (Loretta Carlisle photo.)

display explaining the history of the fort, the installation of the weapons, and their operation.

The guns on display in the emplacements and on the grounds include four 12-inch M1890-M1 mortars as well as two British breech-loading, rapid-fire rifles of 1890 vintage that were added to the site in 1982.

A gift shop and lunch room near the gun emplacements provides snacks, beach gear, and souvenirs.

Things to See Nearby

Fort Dade on the nearby island of Egmont Key is accessible by ferryboat from February 15 to December 15, although only ruins remain at that site. Fort De Soto was administered from Fort Dade from its construction in 1900 until February 1904, and the histories of the two forts are intertwined. During the Seminole Wars, Egmont Key served as one of the embarkation points for those Seminoles being shipped west. Even earlier, it had been the site of a Spanish fishing ranchero.

For beach lovers, the beach at Fort De Soto Park is an attraction in itself.

MacDill Air Force Base, located in Tampa, is a nearby attraction of military interest. Air shows are held yearly in March at MacDill.

History

The War Department built the fort as part of the coastal defense of Florida and the United States in response to the Spanish-American War of 1898. Construction began in 1898, and the fort remained in active service until 1923.

Long before he became well known in the Civil War, Robert E. Lee served as a member of the small detachment of U.S. Army engineers who surveyed the area at the mouth of Tampa Bay. In 1849, they recommended that Mullet and Egmont Keys be fortified to serve as part of the offshore defenses of the seacoast. During the Civil War, the Union stationed troops on both islands to

Tampa became a major departure point for U.S. troops sent to Cuba during the 1898 Spanish-American War. In *A street scene at Tampa City*, the local population welcomes troops as they march from the train station to their transport ship. Fort De Soto was built to protect Tampa Bay from Spanish attack. (An 1898 drawing by William Glackens. Courtesy of the Library of Congress.)

help in the blockade of Tampa Bay. However, after the Civil War the two keys were abandoned. But in 1882, the government officially created military reservations on both Mullet and Egmont Keys.

In 1889, the government set up a quarantine station on Mullet Key, and it was turned over to the Marine Hospital Service. The quarantine station stayed in business as a way station for immigrants landing at Tampa Bay until 1937. In that year, the Public Health Service transferred the quarantine work to Gadsden Point.

The government facility on Mullet Key became Fort De Soto in 1900, operating as a detachment of Fort Dade on Egmont Key. The two posts were to provide emplacements for heavy artillery and mortars to guard Tampa Bay.

The fortifications resulted from the Spanish-American War, fought from April to August 1898. The local railroad magnate and hotel tycoon Henry Plant lobbied for using Tampa Bay as the embarkation point for troops to Cuba during that war on the grounds that it was the closest deepwater port to Cuba in

This 1898 pen and ink drawing captures the chaos of assembling troops and loading horses aboard ship at Tampa. (By William Glackens. Courtesy of the Library of Congress.)

the United States with railroad connections. Officers (including Rough Rider Col. Teddy Roosevelt) stayed at Plant's hotel, the Tampa Bay Hotel, now part of the University of Tampa. Plant's efforts were warmly supported by many Cuban exiles living in Tampa, who applauded the U.S. effort to end Spanish rule of their island.

With the use of Egmont Key as a departure and quarantine return point, the Army installed the heavy mortar emplacement as a coastal defense. Of course, by the time Forts Dade and De Soto were completed, the Spanish-American War was long over, as it lasted only about four months. The construction on Mullet

Key began in 1898, and the gun emplacements were completed in 1906. The two major mortar batteries, each with four of the huge guns, were named Battery Laidley and Battery Bigelow.

Battery Laidley was named after U.S. Army Col. T. S. Laidley, who had served in both the Mexican War and the Civil War. Battery Bigelow was named for U.S. Army Lt. Aaron Bigelow, killed at the Battle of Lundy's Lane, in Ontario, Canada, in 1814, during the War of 1812 between the United States and Great Britain.

The 12-inch mortars, behind the walls of concrete and sand dunes, were invisible to incoming ships, and the crews could fire the weapons from the protected position. The seaward walls are 16 feet thick, while the landward side walls are 8 feet thick. The roof over the magazine rooms is 5 feet thick.

The guns were never fired in battle, but used only for target practice. A steamship would tow a target, and spotters would relay target information by telephone to a "data booth" that can be seen behind the gun emplacements. The targeting information would be posted on a slate board and read to the gun crews.

Although the weapons had an electric firing mechanism, rather than a mechanical lanyard (rope-pull), the guns were swiveled or elevated by hand, by turning wheels. The guns are 161 inches long and had a 12-inch bore. The powder charges were nitro-cellulose, either 65 pounds, for maximum range, or 48 pounds for shorter range. Maximum range, at a 45-degree angle of elevation and with the heavy charge, would take the shell 6.8 miles down range. It could penetrate 6 inches of steel armor. After the guns fired 250 rounds, the inner barrel core would have to be replaced. The mortars were a great advance over prior heavy mortars in that they were all-steel construction; previous mortars had cast-iron cores.

The mortars themselves were manufactured at the Watervliet Arsenal in New York, and the gun carriages were made by the American Hoist and Derrick Company of St. Paul, Minnesota.

The Army added two 3-inch Driggs-Seabury rapid-fire artillery pieces, capable of firing 15-pound shot to a range of 4.5 miles. These direct-fire weapons were later removed, and the two guns installed on the grounds behind the batteries in 1982 represent

This gun was installed on the grounds at Fort De Soto in 1982 to represent the breech-loading weapons used in close-in defense against destroyers and other ships. (Loretta Carlisle photo.)

the type of weapon used for such close-in defense against destroyers.

In addition to the gun emplacements, there were twenty-nine buildings on the post, including an administration building, a large barracks, a hospital, a guardhouse, and workshops. Brick roads, a narrow-gauge railroad, and concrete sidewalks provided transportation routes through the base. The rail line ran from a wharf to the storage facilities, with a spur line to the mortar emplacements. An overhead cable line supplemented the rail line for transportation of supplies around the base.

The Army nearly abandoned the base in 1910, with only a skeleton crew of caretakers remaining, including just a sergeant and a game warden. During 1917–18, when the United States was involved in World War I, a slightly larger team of troops maintained the fort. In 1917, four of the heavy mortars were taken apart and shipped to San Diego, California.

In the concrete bunkers behind the heavy mortars, a display of photographs from the early history of the fort convey an impression of the drills with the guns and life among the troops.

Both Fort Dade and Fort De Soto were officially abandoned on May 25, 1923, with just a single caretaker at each fort. Over the following years, hurricanes and ordinary storms wreaked havoc on the wooden structures of both forts, leaving behind only the heavy concrete structures. The Army tried to sell the post, and finally, in 1938, Pinellas County bought Fort De Soto. However, by 1940, with the war clouds of World War II gathering, the War Department decided to repurchase the land to use as a bombing range.

In June 1941, the War Department purchased the key from Pinellas County and attached it to MacDill Air Field as part of the practice target range. Paul Tibbets, who piloted the *Enola Gay,* which dropped the atomic bomb on Hiroshima in 1945, practiced with sand-filled bombs at Mullet Key. Fighter pilots in training strafed the island from P-40s and P-51s. Bombing of targets on Mullet Key was restricted to 250-pound bombs; larger ones caused window damage in St. Petersburg.

After World War II, in 1948, Pinellas County once again bought the key, and since then it has remained part of the county lands.

This "supply clerk" greets visitors at the museum at Fort De Soto, where displays present the history of the fort and its role through the twentieth century. (Loretta Carlisle photo.)

In 1962, a toll road was built out to the island, the Pinellas Bayway (SR 682). The county opened the park on December 21, 1962, and officially dedicated it on May 11, 1963. One existing building, the rebuilt quartermaster storehouse, now serves as the "Quartermaster Storehouse Museum," housing a display giving the history of both Fort De Soto and Fort Dade. The museum display contains many informative panels relating to the early history of the fort and especially to the use of De Soto as a bombing range in World War II.

The building originally housed the Post Exchange, and it served as a warehouse for supplies from 1905 to 1910, when the troops transferred from Fort De Soto to Fort Morgan in Alabama. The Army abandoned plans then under way to convert the building to a bowling alley. The building fell into ruin, and volunteers carefully rebuilt the present building with funding from both Pinellas County and the Florida Department of State, following pictures and plans of the original storehouse.

The National Register of Historic Places listed the remaining 12-inch mortar batteries in 1978.

4 South Florida

20

East and West Martello Towers

Location: *East Tower*: near airport at 3501 Roosevelt Blvd., Key West. *West Tower*: at the intersection of White Street and Atlantic Avenue, on Higgs Beach.
Driving Directions: The towers are 3 and 1.5 miles east of Fort Zachary Taylor on the south shore of Key West. *The East Tower* is about 2 miles along Roosevelt Boulevard from the intersection of US 1. *The West Tower* can be reached by following Roosevelt Boulevard west along the beachfront, jogging right and then left onto Atlantic Boulevard, and following Atlantic to White Street and Higgs Beach. The West Tower is on the beach side of the road.
Hours of Operation: East Tower: 9 a.m. to 4:30 p.m. daily. West Tower: 9:30 a.m. to 3:15 p.m. daily. Call ahead as hours may change from season to season.
Fees: East Tower: $6 per person (seniors, $5). West Tower: No admission charge; donations accepted.
Phone: East Tower: (305) 296-3913; rental of the facility and grounds for special events can be arranged. West Tower: (305) 294-3210; rental of the facility for weddings and other special events can be scheduled at Webmaster@keywestgardenclub.com.

Unique Facts

Martello towers are unique gun towers, so named after such towers built in Italy. The two in Key West are the only surviving

examples of Martello towers in the United States, although several can be found in Canada—in Quebec, Nova Scotia, and elsewhere. Although most Martello towers in Europe and elsewhere are round, the two in Key West are square.

Things to See

The East Tower is maintained by the Key West Art and Historical Society and has both a permanent display of historical artifacts in the exterior casemates of the surrounding fort walls and, on the second floor of the central tower, an art gallery with permanent gallery shows. The view from the top of the tower is one of the most spectacular in Key West.

The West Tower, which suffered from being used for target practice, is a ruin. However, details of the construction can still be seen both from the inside and outside; the West Tower is maintained by the Key West Garden Club, and the grounds provide a sampling of the luxuriant vegetation found in the Keys.

Noteworthy are the casemate rooms for emplacement of guns, the outer defensive walls, and the brick construction itself. In

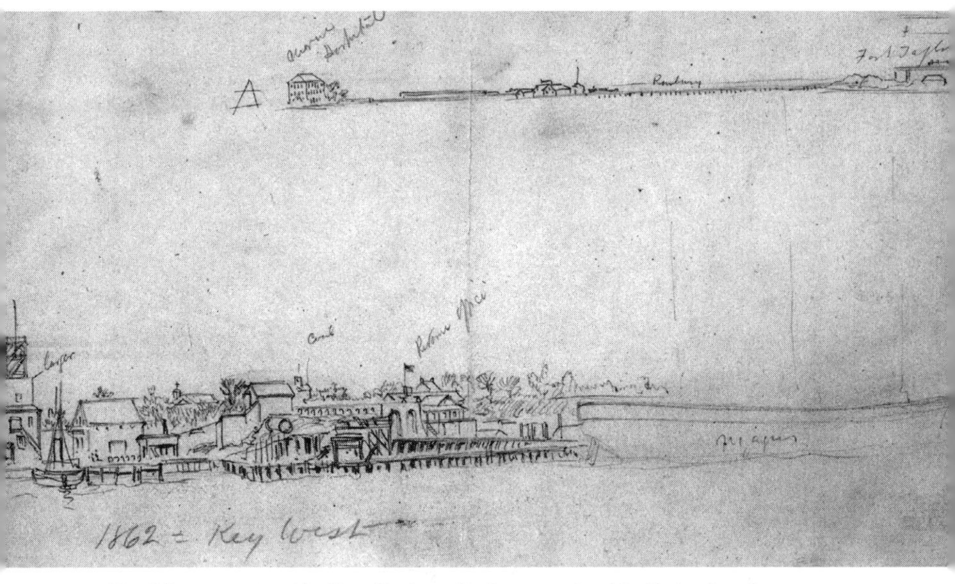

Key West, protected by Fort Zachary Taylor, remained in Union hands during the Civil War. (Drawing by Alfred R. Waud, 1862. Courtesy of the Library of Congress.)

The entrance to the East Martello Tower sometimes advertises Key West's ghost heritage. (Loretta Carlisle photo.)

The Key West Garden Club maintains a display at the West Martello Tower, including this ficus (fig) tree that almost completely conceals the ruined masonry of the tower. (Loretta Carlisle photo.)

both forts, interior concrete aggregate incorporating shells formed cores, overlaid with brick walls. Because of the destruction at the West Tower, the ruined walls demonstrate this brick-over-aggregate method of construction.

Things to See Nearby

Nearby military sites of interest include Fort Zachary Taylor and the Truman Little White House. The town of Key West contains many historical sites of interest, most notably the Ernest Hemingway Home.

History

The Army originally built the two towers beginning in 1863 as part of the defenses of the port of Key West that included Fort Zachary Taylor. The commandant at Fort Taylor had jurisdiction over the two towers. Original planning had included two more Martello towers that were never built. The Army abandoned the West Tower in 1866, and the East Tower in 1873. A rail line ran from Fort Taylor to connect the two towers to Fort Taylor. The central towers at each location allowed the emplacement of guns that could fire in any direction, surrounded by an outer wall that would make the small forts practically invulnerable to attack.

The development of exploding shells, which could readily break up brick structures, made the forts obsolete even as they were being completed, so neither ever had full-scale armaments. The Army installed two small cannon in the West Tower in the 1880s.

Both towers lay abandoned for years. In 1947, the U.S. Army released the two towers to the Monroe County commissioners, and released Fort Taylor to the Navy. The towers fell into disrepair. Gunners at Fort Taylor had lobbed a few practice rounds at the West Tower, and later, some local people "mined" the towers for bricks to use in walkways and other structures. In 1951, the Key West Art and Historical Society took over the East Tower and restored it to provide a museum setting. The Key West Garden

The original local cement, incorporating seashells, can be seen in this ruined section of the West Martello Tower. (Loretta Carlisle photo.)

At the East Martello Tower in Key West, the Art and Historical Society maintains a display that includes this walk-in playhouse. (Loretta Carlisle photo.)

Club took over the West Tower in 1955. The towers were preserved from destruction through the efforts of State Representative Joe Allen. In his memory, the West Tower has been renamed the Joe Allen Art and Garden Center.

The East Tower's casemates, citadel, and courtyard now provide the setting for a large collection of Key West artifacts and historical records as well as good examples of military memorabilia and equipment. From the top of the central tower, a 360-degree view gives a beautiful panorama of the Atlantic coast of Key West. In the East Tower garden, there is an eighty-year-old playhouse that shows visitors how children played in old Key West.

The art galleries in the East Tower citadel display Florida's largest collections of painted wood carvings and drawings by the Key West artist Mario Sanchez and the scrap metal "junk" sculpture of Stanley Papio, another renowned local folk artist. Papio had worked as a roustabout, wrestler, and welder. During the early to mid-twentieth century, he created a series of constructions that he welded together from scrap metal that he recovered from junk autos, appliances, and other discarded iron and steel. The sculptures sometimes took the form of portraits of individual people, while others represent fanciful beasts. He did the welding and painting at his home and displayed the works in his yard in the upper Keys.

Robert the Haunted Doll

Among the collections are numerous interesting items, including "Robert the haunted doll." The subject of great interest by students of the paranormal, the doll served as the basis for an urban legend. The story started in the nineteenth century: the doll, a cloth figurine stuffed with straw, belonged to the Key West artist Robert Eugene Otto, known as "Gene." Otto received the toy as a child, when he and his family lived in the mansion at the corner of Eaton and Simonton Streets, in a building now known as the Artist House. That building has become a regular stop on local "ghost tours." In the late 1800s, Otto and the doll became

Legends surrounding Robert the Haunted Doll have been the subject of several books and television specials. The doll is on display in the East Martello Tower. Ask permission of the doll before taking his picture! (Loretta Carlisle photo.)

too close for his parents' taste, with the boy often blaming the doll for strange events and broken items. It seems that Gene's father, Thomas, was hard on the servants, and one of them, known for his knowledge of West Indian voodoo, provided Gene with the "Robert" doll and planted the idea of its taking blame for problems.

When Gene's parents heard him talking to the doll in the upstairs bedroom, it seemed natural enough. Kids do that sort of thing. But then they could hear the doll answering in an entirely different voice!

The doll eventually began to frighten even Gene's best friends, so Otto's parents relegated the Robert doll to an attic room. Legend has it that Robert the Doll did not like his exile to the attic, though, and that he would taunt schoolchildren from the window as they walked past the house. Some of them, so the story goes, became so frightened that they eventually walked out of their way to avoid the doll on their way to and from school.

When Gene Otto inherited the house from his parents, he reunited with Robert the Doll and brought him back downstairs. Once again, Robert began catching the blame for problems, much to the annoyance of Otto's wife. She returned the doll to the attic, where it remained until Otto died in 1974. Even after the owners sold the home, the doll continued its antics, scaring the wits out of the new owners, with reports of the doll rocking by itself in a chair and giggling eerily in the night. The museum staff have a few more tales to tell of Robert's continued behavior, even when on display. They wryly inform visitors that they are welcome to take pictures of Robert, but they should ask his permission first.

21

Fort Zachary Taylor

Location: Key West
Driving Directions: At the end of Southard Street through the Truman Annex.
Hours of Operation: 8 a.m. until sundown, 365 days a year.
Fees: $6 per vehicle (limit 8 people per vehicle). $2 for pedestrians, bicyclists, extra passengers, passengers in vehicle with holder of Annual Individual Entrance Pass. $4 for single-occupant vehicle or motorcycle. There is an additional 50-cent-per-person Monroe County surcharge on each admission fee.
Phone: (305) 292-6713
Special Events: Annual sculpture show, January through April. Reenactments, fourth weekend in February.

Unique Facts

Through the Civil War, the Union held only three forts in the Confederate States throughout the duration of the war: Fort Jefferson in the Dry Tortugas, Fort Pickens off Pensacola, and Fort Zachary Taylor in Key West. None of these three forts ever fell to the Confederate Army or secessionist state militias. The view of the sunset from Fort Zachary Taylor is the only unobstructed view in Key West. The fort is the southernmost park in the Florida State Park system.

This sketch shows the interior of Fort Taylor in the 1860s. (Attributed to Alfred R. Waud; possibly by William Waud. Courtesy of the Library of Congress.)

Every year Key West puts on a sculpture show with display venues throughout the town. This display occupies the outer grounds of Fort Zachary Taylor. (Loretta Carlisle photo.)

Things to See

The fort has one of the largest displays of Civil War–era cannons in the United States and one of the largest collections of Spanish-American War artifacts. The brick construction is typical of the Third System of Fortifications–type fort. The "Fort Zach" beach is a popular spot for snorkeling and swimming, with a shaded area of picnic tables close to the beach.

A 45-minute guided tour is provided, as well as self-guided tours. The guided tours begin at noon and 2 p.m. daily. Canoes and kayaks can be launched in a designated area. Bicycling or walking along a nature trail is allowed. The fort is a popular site for weddings, which can be scheduled through the Visitor Service Provider's event service: (305) 295-0033.

The Visitor Service Provider maintains a shop and lunchroom with an extended menu, beachfront dining, rentals of beach equipment, and a gift shop. During winter sculpture exhibitions, the exterior grounds of the fort become part of the citywide sculpture display.

Things to See Nearby

Nearby military historical sites of interest include two Martello towers in Key West that were originally administered from Fort Zachary Taylor, as well as Fort Jefferson (available by boat tour). The Truman Little White House is also of military and political significance, located directly ashore from the fort. Other notable local historical sites include the Ernest Hemingway Home, the Key West Lighthouse Museum, the Oldest House and Garden Museum, the Audubon House and Tropical Gardens, the Shipwreck Historeum, and the Key West Museum of Art and History in the Custom House. The many shops, restaurants, and unique genre architecture of Key West are themselves attractions. At the foot of Simonton Street, as one drives into the fort complex, the USS *Mohawk*, a World War II–vintage Coast Guard cutter, is docked and is open for visiting.

History

The fort was originally built beginning in the 1840s, and the Army altered it over the years, removing some of the outer wall facing on the landward side. The original construction of the side of the fort facing the ocean and the inner court are preserved.

In 1845, the U.S. government purchased 62.89 acres from local landowners in Key West for the construction of a fort to protect the harbor of this most southern city in the United States. By November 1845, initial construction began on temporary buildings built of yellow pine. Over the next two decades, yellow fever, hurricanes, and the Civil War itself interrupted construction work. In fact, the first destruction came from a storm just a year after work on the fort began, in 1846, destroying all the buildings except for a blacksmith shop, a stable, and a water cistern. Four workers were drowned.

President Zachary Taylor, elected the twelfth president of the United States in 1848, died July 9, 1850, just sixteen months into his term of office. The fort, still under construction, was named after him.

Further storms in 1850 and 1856 halted construction, but by 1861, the fort neared completion. Built of bricks, the fort followed the "Third System of Fortifications" model similar to that of Fort Clinch (on Amelia Island), Fort Pickens (near Pensacola), and Fort Jefferson (in the Dry Tortugas). That is, it fronted on a major water approach to the United States and had high masonry walls, with a polygonal bastion formation surrounding an inner courtyard. To the extent possible, the forts were built to be self-sufficient and impregnable from land or sea attack with contemporary weapons. When first built, Fort Taylor was surrounded by 10 feet of water at high tide, and stood about 440 yards from shore, making the fort virtually unassailable by land forces. With its high walls and heavy ordnance, the fort could evade bombardment from sea, as the range of its own 8- and 10-inch weapons would exceed those of any warships of the era.

The fort had a trapezoidal shape with the broad base facing the shore and with that side housing the barracks. That landward side had a roof with a series of gabled or projecting windows facing the shore, while the outer walls had flat roofs for gun emplacement. The four corners had bastions, also mounting guns. The underwater foundations were built of granite and coral rock, embedded with concrete. The outer walls were three tiers or stories high; with later reconstruction, the inner floors were removed so the height is now one story. In the period 1898–1905, the Army "modernized" the fort with additions of concrete walls, on a weaker foundation, that included "Battery Osceola" and "Battery Adair." Oddly, a number of Civil War–era guns were used as part of the fill for the foundation of this addition, and excavation has retrieved some of them. Parts of these walls are already dangerously deteriorated, and park officials estimate that the original brick walls will long outlast the concrete walls on these two batteries.

Battery Adair was named for Lt. Lewis Adair of the Twenty-second Infantry, who died of wounds received in the war against the Sioux Indians in the Dakota Territory in 1872. Battery Adair had four rapid-fire guns designed to defend Key West from fast torpedo boats. Battery Osceola is named for the war leader of the

The heavy casemates or gun rooms at Fort Zachary Taylor are typical of the casemates in other Third System of Fortifications forts, like Clinch, Jefferson, and Barrancas. (Loretta Carlisle photo.)

Seminole people, who led resistance to U.S. armed forces in the Second Seminole War. This battery contained two 12-inch rifled cannon that could fire a 1,000-pound shot up to 10 miles.

From the landward side, a 720-foot-long drawbridge connected to the shore before drifting sand filled the intervening water area. Early drawings and engravings of the fort show the narrow bridge leading to the shore, making the fort very readily defended from any attack in that direction, with the bastions clearly able to cover all approaches.

The fort had its own desalinization system for water supply, remains of which can still be seen, and sewer lines flushed by ocean tides. During excavation in the 1960s, investigators found details of the desalinization plant, a patented, French-designed system: "Dr. Normandy's Patent Marine Aerated Fresh Water Apparatus."

The barrack rooms can be seen, together with traverse irons for gun carriages. Among the weapons uncovered were a rifled

Parrott gun, an 1853 Colombian and an 1854 Colombian, and an 8-inch Rodman gun mounted on an 1865 carriage.

At the beginning of the Civil War, the Union War Department purchased land for the two related Martello towers ashore. Located 1.5, and 3.0 miles from Fort Taylor, along the southern shore of Key West, a short rail line connected them to the main fort. The two small tower forts, which would allow the emplacement of guns that could fire in any compass direction over 360 degrees, served as a supplement to the defenses of Key West. This guide covers them in a separate entry.

During the Civil War, the fort remained in Union hands under the command of U.S. Army Artillery Capt. John Brannan. Some 299 confiscated Confederate blockade-running ships were towed by the blockading U.S. Navy to Key West, and held under the guns of the fort, which was never attacked. Thus the island city remained in Union hands for the duration of the war, the command post for the Union blockade of the Florida coast.

In the storm season of 1865 following the end of the Civil War, a hurricane severely damaged the fort and the two Martello towers in town. Another set of storms in 1875 and 1876 destroyed some of the fort buildings and damaged the bridge.

An 1879 report described the fort as being in severely deteriorated condition. Storms had left leaks in the roof of the barracks, bricks needed to be repointed, and the bridge had become unsafe. During the Spanish-American War of 1898, the Army repaired the fort, with some of the barracks buildings removed to provide a wider access from the landward side. During these repairs, builders greatly altered the fort, removing the third tier and installing "disappearing guns." Officers at the fort operated the minefield protecting the harbor. The fort also stored high explosives, ammunition, and coal. During the Spanish-American War, the Navy brought some thirty-four captured Spanish ships into the port of Key West, and the United States confined some four hundred Spanish prisoners in the fort rather than aboard vessels in the harbor. Sand filled the shallow lagoon behind the fort so that it was no longer located on an island, but connected by a wide spit of curving beach to the shore.

Fort Zachary Taylor was originally reached by a long causeway and bridge; but later landfill left the fort isolated from Key West by only a moat. (Loretta Carlisle photo.)

In 1947, the Army transferred the fort to the jurisdiction of the Navy. Over the following twenty years, the Navy used the fort for the storage of surplus gear, before turning it over, in 1968, for restoration by the State of Florida as part of the state park system. In that year, a group of volunteers led by Howard S. England uncovered some of the Civil War–era guns and ammunition buried within the fort sands.

The National Register of Historic Places listed Fort Taylor in 1971, and the fort became a National Historic Landmark in 1973. A moat dug around the landward side of the fort in 1989 restored an element of its early appearance. The fort park now occupies 87 acres including filled-in areas as well as an attractive picnic and bathing beach.

The Harry Truman Annex was originally part of the fort, and it now includes a residential neighborhood of Key West. When the Navy took over the fort in 1947, it added the landward section as an "annex" to the Key West Naval Station. Docks at the annex waterfront housed submarines until the advent of larger nuclear submarines by the 1970s made the harbor too shallow for those craft.

Although most of the annex land became private property in a gated community, 32.4 acres were transferred to the City of Key West to preserve Harry Truman's winter home—The Truman Little White House—where he spent 175 days as president in the period 1945–52. The Truman Little White House is discussed in the next entry in this guide. The whole section, including the private homes on former Navy land, as well as the Truman Little White House, is now known as the Harry Truman Annex.

22

Truman Little White House

Location: Key West

Driving Directions: In the Truman Annex at westernmost edge of the town. The gate into the Truman Annex most appropriate for foot traffic is at Caroline and Whitehead Streets. Proceed through the gate and walk to Front Street. The Truman Little White House is dead-ahead. There is paid parking on Whitehead Street. An alternative, free-parking site that entails a slightly longer walk is at the end of Southard Street in the lot in front of the USS *Mohawk*. On foot, proceed back up Southard to Front Street and turn left. The Truman Little White House is four blocks along Front Street, on the left.

Hours of Operation: 9 a.m. to 4:30 p.m. Tours begin every 20 minutes, 365 days a year. The store and gift shop is open until 5 p.m.

Fees: $15 per person if purchased online.

Phone: (305) 294-9911

Website: www.trumanlittlewhitehouse.com/key-west/historic-home-museum-tour.htm

Note: All parking in the Truman Annex is prohibited. The nearest paid parking is at the Westin Resort, 245 Front Street (about 500 feet) or on Whitehead Street.

This building was originally a duplex for officer housing at the Key West Naval Station, but it was converted to a single-family residence that served as a vacation home for President Harry S. Truman. (Loretta Carlisle photo.)

Special Events

Special events, conferences, symposia, and other events are scheduled from time to time so it is important to call ahead to verify that the house is open for tour. Weddings and wedding receptions can be planned for the grounds, usually beginning at 6 p.m. after the regular closing hours; events are scheduled through the event planner at (305) 294-9911.

Unique Facts

President Harry S. Truman regarded this home as his favorite winter vacation spot from 1946 through 1953; other presidents have visited and stayed in the structure before and since that time.

Things to See

Knowledgeable volunteer guides take visitors on a tour of the building and museum. The grounds surrounding the home are parklike. The front lawn, with tall palms and enormous tropical almond trees, is a favorite locale for Key West wedding ceremonies. The side lawn is shaded by a variety of specimen tropical shade trees, and the rear lawn is open and spacious. White-painted wooden Adirondack chairs are available on the lawns.

Things to See Nearby

Accessed through the Truman Annex, Fort Zachary Taylor lies immediately to the west. Other nearby military and historical sites of interest include: USS *Mohawk* (a World War II–era U.S. Coast Guard cutter), two Martello towers in Key West, which were historically administered from Fort Zachary Taylor, as well as Fort Jefferson (accessible by boat tour). Other notable local historical sites include the Ernest Hemingway Home, the Key West Lighthouse Museum, the Oldest House and Garden Museum, the Audubon House and Tropical Gardens, and the Key West Museum of Art and History in the Custom House. The many shops, restaurants, and unique genre architecture of Key West are themselves attractions.

History

The Navy originally built the house in 1890 on the waterfront as a two-family dwelling for the naval base commandant and the paymaster. As a two-family residence, the structure was known as Quarters A and B. Its first significant historic role was to serve as Navy command headquarters during the Spanish-American War, especially for the campaign in Cuba and the Caribbean. Adm. William Peary (famous for Arctic exploration) designed the actual waterfront seawall. The original seawall stretched parallel to the house, just about six or eight feet directly behind the building.

The naval base harbor was dredged in 1909 to accommodate the larger ships being built in that era, and the land in front of the residence was filled in with some of the material dredged from the basin. The two-family structure was converted into a

These Adirondack chairs on the grounds of the Truman Little White House are identical to those used by Harry Truman in the 1940s. (Loretta Carlisle photo.)

single-family home in 1911, and the first U.S. president to visit the facility was William Howard Taft, in December 1912, after he had been defeated for reelection by Woodrow Wilson. By 2011, a total of seven U.S. presidents or former presidents had visited the Truman Little White House.

Through its first fifty years, the house remained the official residence of the base commander. The scientist Edward Hayden served as base commander from 1910 to 1911 and 1912 to 1915, and lived in the house while engaged in hurricane research. Hayden had gained fame for having published a scientific study of hurricanes, *West Indian Hurricanes and the March Blizzard, 1888.*

In World War I, the inventor Thomas Edison lived here for six months while working on methods of locating U-boats and camouflaging merchant ships for the war effort.

During World War II, the Key West Naval Station was heavily involved as a submarine base in protecting Allied shipping in the Straits of Florida. Among special naval outfits at the base in the period were the Fleet Sonar School, the Underwater Swimmers

School (for scuba training), and the Underwater Explosives School. Detachments at the naval base included surface craft and the naval air station as well as the submarine base. However, with the construction of larger submarines beginning in the postwar era, the base could not accommodate them, and that facility was phased out.

Beginning in November 1946, President Truman began visiting the house for winter vacations, logging 175 days there altogether. On Truman's first visit, the base commander took up residence in other quarters on the base. The building became known as the "Winter White House" or the "Little White House" during Truman's administration, which lasted to 1953.

Altogether, Truman spent eleven working vacations here. An important set of documents coming out of Truman's eleven trips were the official trip logs. Sometimes thought of as mere souvenirs for family and staff, the logs give vital clues about the work the president did while staying in Key West. Among the crucial events and meetings that took place in the building, the most significant from a military point of view was a 1948 meeting of the joint chiefs of staff. Out of the meeting came the decision to create the Department of Defense by merging the Department of War and Department of the Navy; Truman signed the Defense Unification Act at a desk that still bears his famous "The Buck Stops Here" sign.

Other crucial decisions and policies emerged from Truman's winter stays at the Little White House. Here he discussed the Marshall Plan to rebuild Europe and the Truman Doctrine that changed American foreign policy and marked the beginning of U.S. military support for democratic, anticommunist regimes in Europe. He decided on the immediate recognition of the independence of the State of Israel in 1948. In this building, he wrote his fourth Civil Rights Executive Order requiring that federal contractors hire minorities. He drafted a letter that called for a two-week cease-fire in Korea. The reaction of Gen. Douglas MacArthur to this letter led to his dismissal as the Allied commander. Even though Truman claimed he was on vacation while at the Little White House, he admitted to officially signing his name two hundred to six hundred times a day during one visit.

In 1952, the U.S. Navy temporarily redivided the Little White House into a duplex known as Quarters A & B, just as it had been in its first years. The naval station commander lived in Quarters A until 1957, when the Navy converted the entire building back into a single dwelling again. The commander of the submarine base (as distinct from the naval station commander) lived in other quarters after 1946.

In retirement from the presidency, former president Truman made five visits to Key West between 1957 and 1969. Each time he came, he visited the Truman Little White House to recall fond memories of his stays there, but he stayed in a private residence in town during these trips.

Visits from Other Presidents and Dignitaries

Other presidents have visited and used the house. The west quarters are now kept as a VIP suite, and visiting dignitaries pay rent to stay there, which helps support the maintenance of the structure. President Dwight Eisenhower held meetings there in December 1955 and January 1956 while recuperating from a heart attack. President John F. Kennedy used the building for a summit meeting with British prime minister Harold Macmillan on March 26, 1961, just twenty-three days before the Bay of Pigs invasion of Cuba. Kennedy returned to the Truman Little White House on November 26, 1962, following the Cuban Missile Crisis, for an inspection tour.

Other dignitary visits included one in April 1972 by King Hussein I of Jordan, who came as a guest of RADM John Maurer. In 1996, President Jimmy and Mrs. Rosalyn Carter used the house for a family gathering. On April 2–6, 2001, Secretary of State Colin Powell opened peace talks in this house between the presidents of Armenia and Azerbaijan. Behind the structure, a series of flagpoles bear the flags of the participating nations in that meeting. In 2005, President Bill Clinton and then senator Hillary

Clinton used the house as a weekend retreat. In December 2007, former president Jimmy Carter came back for another family visit, bringing a large number of Carter children and grandchildren along.

The guided tour of the Truman Little White House focuses on anecdotes and details of Truman's stays at the structure, and includes many fascinating details regarding Truman's personal traits, his daily schedule, and the important decisions taken at the structure.

The Truman Annex

The Navy base land surrounding the former commandant's home was named the Truman Annex in 1973 following the death of President Truman in December 1972. The U.S. Department of the Interior listed the Truman Little White House on the National Register of Historic Places on February 12, 1974.

Key West Naval Station was formerly disestablished on March 29, 1974. Over the period 1974–86, the building stood empty, in caretaker status until it, along with 43 acres of the Naval Station, was sold. The sale took place at a public auction on September 10, 1986, to private developer Pritam Singh for $17.25 million, which he paid for the whole section of land in the Truman Annex Naval Station including the Little White House and the surrounding acreage. Mr. Singh, based in Maine, transferred title to the house and its gardens to the State of Florida on January 1, 1987, and the state holds the house in trust.

Over the period 1987–90, Mr. Singh directed and funded the restoration of the building and the grounds, being careful to restore the building to its condition and style during the Truman era. Mr. and Mrs. Henry Drettman of Grosse Point, Michigan, provided further major funding during the 1990s. In 1999, Historic Tours of America, a private firm headquartered in Key West, signed an agreement with the State of Florida to continue the restoration and became a major donor and corporate sponsor of the site.

23

Fort Jefferson

Location: Fort Jefferson is built on a low-lying island, or key, in the Dry Tortugas. It is located on Garden Key within the Dry Tortugas National Park, about 70 miles due west of the island of Key West. It can only be reached by ferry, private boat, or seaplane. The map coordinates of Fort Jefferson are 24°37'41"N by 82°52'23"W. For travel by private boat, U.S. Coast Guard and Geodetic Survey Chart #11438 is used for navigation to the Dry Tortugas. Two public boat lines provide daily visits to the fort, with departures from Key West in the morning and return to Key West late in the afternoon.
Hours of Operation: Fort Jefferson, operated by the National Park Service, is open during daylight hours year-round.
Fees: $5 admission charge. Reservations for ferry or seaplane services should be arranged in advance of any planned trip. The ferry trip takes about 2 hours from Key West and costs in the range of $130 to $150 per person, with brunch and luncheon served.
Phone: (305) 242-7700
Ferry Services: *Sunny Days*: (800) 236-7937 or (305) 292-6100; www.drytortugas.com. *Yankee Fleet*: (800) 634-0939 or (305) 294-7009; www.yankeefleet.com.
Air Services: *Seaplanes of Key West*. For schedules, prices, and reservations: (800) 950-2FLY (2359) or (305) 294-0709; www.seaplanesof keywest.com.

Unique Facts

The islands were discovered in 1513 by Ponce de León, who named them Las Tortugas, Spanish for "The Turtles," for the abundant sea turtles found in the low-lying keys. English-speaking sailors soon called them the Dry Tortugas, to serve as a warning that no freshwater was available on the keys.

Fort Jefferson is one of only three U.S. Army forts located in the Confederacy that were never taken over or seized by Confederate troops; the other two were Fort Pickens and Fort Zachary Taylor. All three are in Florida. A fourth fort, Fort Sumter, in Charleston harbor, remained in Federal hands after the formation of the Confederacy; South Carolina and Confederate bombardment to subdue that fort initiated the Civil War on April 13, 1861. As noted in the entry for Fort Clinch, Confederate forces briefly occupied that fort.

Fort Jefferson was constructed from approximately 16 million bricks, making it the largest brick structure in the Western Hemisphere (since so much of the 21-million-brick Fort Pickens was

After a two-hour trip by high-speed ferry, visitors greet this welcome sign at the entrance to the fort on Garden Key in the Dry Tortugas, some 70 miles from Key West. (Loretta Carlisle photo.)

This iron lighthouse at Fort Jefferson was built in 1877 to replace an older one on the island. (Loretta Carlisle photo.)

destroyed). The Battersea Power Station in London, the Stockport railway viaduct in Britain, and the Castle of Malbork, about 29 miles from Gdansk in Poland, all lay claim to being larger brick structures.

At Fort Jefferson, a display of six 15-inch Rodman guns is the largest collection of Rodman guns in the world.

Things to See

The fort has many features typical of the Third System of Fortifications that are interesting to see, including gun casemates (gun rooms) with their slanted openings or embrasures, Rodman cannons, the moat and moat wall, an iron lighthouse, as well as the magnificent blue waters of the Gulf of Mexico.

There are excellent opportunities for photography. Snorkeling in the shallow waters of the keys and bird-watching outside the fort are spectacular; eleven primitive camping spots are available. Campsites are available on a first-come basis; reservations are required and may be made by calling 1-888-382-7864. On a clear night, with no light pollution from nearby cities, the starry sky is beautiful.

A self-guided tour of the fort provided by the Park Service takes about 45 minutes, but many visitors take more time. Guides from the tour boats also provide guided tours. Among other noteworthy sites at the fort is the cell that once held Dr. Samuel Mudd, implicated in the plot to assassinate Abraham Lincoln. The iron shutters—known as Totten shutters—that once covered the gun ports or embrasures offer another point of interest. Designed by Gen. Joseph Gilbert Totten (1788–1864), after whom Fort Totten in New York was named, these shutters would swing open as a gun fired, blown out from the blast of air from the gun, allowing the cannonball to pass unobstructed. After the shot fired, the shutters would swing closed, protecting the gun

From inside Fort Jefferson, the ragged gun port provides a view of the moat. The ports are irregular because the iron Totten shutters, designed to protect the gunners from musket fire, have nearly all rusted out. (Loretta Carlisle photo.)

port from enemy fire. Unfortunately, as the salty, wet air rusted the shutters, they expanded to almost twice their original size, shattering many of the embrasures and almost "exploding" the brickwork around the openings. This damage accounts for the large and often ragged open spaces found in the outer wall of the fort.

Things to See Nearby

The many points of interest in Key West include these military sites:

- Fort Zachary Taylor
- East and West Martello Towers
- Truman Little White House

History

Surveys and Construction

In the period December 1824 to January 1825, U.S. Navy Commodore David Porter made an inspection and survey trip to the Dry Tortugas as part of the Navy's assessment of possible sites for defenses of the newly acquired Florida Territory (which had just been taken over from Spain in 1821). Piracy in the Caribbean had increased greatly during the early 1820s as former privateers from the newly independent Latin American republics turned from privateering (under commissions or letters of mark from the republics) to independent, often murderous attacks on U.S. and European merchant ships. Porter hoped to find an appropriate spot for a naval station or base from which to launch operations against the pirates. Porter was not impressed with the Dry Tortugas, however, and recommended against constructing a fort there.

He reported to the secretary of the Navy that the eleven keys of the Dry Tortugas were unsuitable for a navy base. The lack of freshwater, the small acreage, barely above sea level in calm water, and their sandy base all seemed unsuitable. However, as an aid to navigation, a brick lighthouse and small lighthouse-keeper's cottage were constructed in 1825–26 on Bush Key (later renamed Garden Key).

In 1829, Commodore John Rodgers made an inspection trip to the Dry Tortugas, and he delivered a far more positive report on the keys' suitability for a fort. He believed that the reefs and sandbanks would provide a deep inner anchorage, safe even during storms, and deep enough for major U.S. warships. Furthermore, he pointed out that if an enemy power seized the Dry Tortugas, they would be able to dominate shipping throughout the eastern Gulf.

Rodgers's report and encouragement languished in the Washington bureaucracy for years, but in 1846, construction of Fort Jefferson began on Garden Key, surrounding the 1826 lighthouse and lighthouse-keeper's cottage. The original lighthouse survived fifty years, to be replaced by a metal light tower in 1877, which now stands prominently above the fort's walls. In 1850, the fort, still under construction, was named after President Thomas Jefferson (1801–9). Many shiploads of brick came from Mobile, Alabama, and Pensacola, Florida, while guns and ammunition arrived from the navy yard in Washington, D.C., and from industrial cities of the Northeast.

This Civil War–period sketch by an unidentified artist appears to represent Fort Jefferson in the Dry Tortugas. (Courtesy of the Library of Congress.)

Like Castillo de San Marcos, Fort Jefferson also maintained a hot-shot oven where cannonballs were heated to red-hot before being fired at attacking wooden ships. The shot would ignite the ship or, on a lucky hit, detonate the ship's powder magazine. (Loretta Carlisle photo.)

The fort design followed the Third System of Fortifications model, that is, with high, thick masonry walls pierced by gun ports or embrasures. In this case, it was easy to surround the outside wall with a water-filled moat. The fort is six-sided, with four sides at 477 feet in length, and two at 325 feet. As in some other forts of the era, the walls meet in sharp corners, known as bastions, allowing for defenders to command the approaches to the walls. In addition to the Totten shutters, mentioned above, another feature of the fort was the effort to build cisterns that would collect rainwater. Unfortunately, most of the cisterns leaked, and water had to be brought in by ship for the fort's garrison.

The casemates were built to house 420 heavy guns. The largest, 15-inch Rodman guns weighed up to 25 tons, and could fire a shot up to three miles. The guns were manned by U.S. Army troops, rather than shore-based sailors; however, the guns were never fired in a military engagement.

The walls surrounded a parade ground that housed separate buildings for storehouses, barracks, and thirty-seven powder magazines. Prominent features in the current parade ground are an arched powder magazine (now inhabited by an owl), and a shot furnace with sloping racks to heat shot red-hot.

In addition to skilled carpenters, blacksmiths, and masons, a crew of slaves was hired from private owners to work on the construction. On July 10, 1847, seven slaves made a daring escape from the fort by seizing all the boats on the island to delay pursuit. After scuttling or disabling three of the boats, they sailed the fourth one, a schooner named *Union*, to the east, past Key West, finally coming ashore at Key Vaca (now Marathon Key). However, they were recaptured as they tried to flee. Two of the seven were sent to their owners on shore, while the five others were returned to Fort Jefferson. This little-known episode of freedom seeking has been thoroughly researched by Park Service historians.

By the time of the Civil War, convict laborers replaced the slaves to continue the construction. Even with the years of work from 1846 through the Civil War, the fort was never completely finished.

The Civil War Period and Dr. Mudd

During the Civil War, Fort Jefferson, with its reputation as the "Gibraltar of the Gulf," was never attacked by Confederate ships. The fort served as a prison, not for Confederate prisoners of war, but rather for Union Army deserters and soldiers convicted by court-martial for crimes while in service. In addition, after June 1865, the fort held as prisoners four of the men convicted by military tribunal in the assassination plot that killed Abraham

Lincoln and wounded Secretary of State William Seward. Although John Wilkes Booth, who shot Lincoln, was killed when he refused to surrender, eight others were tried for conspiracy in a military court. Four were executed, but Dr. Samuel Mudd, Samuel Arnold, and Michael O'Laughlen were sentenced to life in prison while Edmund Spangler was sentenced to six years in prison. Mudd, Arnold, O'Laughlen, and Spangler were sent to Fort Jefferson, where they joined the military prisoners serving various terms at hard labor.

In 1867, following the Civil War, a yellow-fever epidemic swept the prison, and supply and relief ships stood offshore, carefully avoiding contact with the contagion. O'Laughlen died from the disease. Dr. Mudd ministered to the sick, earning the respect of fellow prisoners, guards, and officers at the prison. President Andrew Johnson pardoned Mudd, Spangler, and Arnold in the last weeks of his term in office, in February 1869. Dr. Mudd's cell is open for tour, at the first corner bastion to the right (viewed from inside) of the entrance to the fort parade ground.

A continuing controversy surrounded the issue of whether Dr. Mudd was actually guilty of conspiracy, although numerous pieces of historical evidence point to the fact that he worked with John Wilkes Booth prior to the assassination, planning to assist in the kidnapping of the president. The expression "His name is Mudd" is said to derive from the story of how Dr. Mudd's reputation was damaged by his conviction.

Later Years

Following several hurricanes, the U.S. Army abandoned the fort in 1874. The fort remained uncompleted, although the original lighthouse was replaced in 1877 and continually manned. From 1888 through 1900, the fort served as a quarantine station, administered by the Marine-Hospital Service. The Navy took over the fort in 1898, using the Dry Tortugas anchorage as a staging area for the invasion of Cuba during the Spanish-American War in that year. Troops of the Twenty-fifth Infantry (the African

American unit known as the Buffalo Soldiers) were stationed there prior to being sent to Cuba. During World War I (1917–18), troops were stationed briefly at the fort.

In 1908, the islands of the Dry Tortugas were designated as a bird reserve and transferred to the Department of Agriculture. After a visit by yacht, President Franklin D. Roosevelt designated the fort and the Dry Tortugas as the Fort Jefferson National Monument on January 4, 1935. It was the first group of offshore islands to be made into a National Monument. On October 26, 1992, President George H. W. Bush signed an act that upgraded the status of the fort and the surrounding keys from National Monument to National Park.

Chronology

1513—During exploration of Florida, Ponce de León discovers the Dry Tortugas islands, which later become the site of Fort Jefferson.

1528—Spanish explorer Pánfilo de Narváez passes through West Florida, camping near the site of present Fort San Marcos de Apalache; he builds a ship, thought to be the first ever constructed by Europeans on mainland North America.

1539—Explorer Hernando de Soto stops near site of Fort San Marcos de Apalache.

1559–61—Spanish expedition under Don Tristan de Luna y Arellano fails to establish a permanent settlement at Pensacola.

1562, May 2—French officer Jean Ribault erects monument near site where Fort Caroline would be built, overlooking the River of May (present-day St. Johns River).

1564, June 22—René Goulaine de Laudonnière, with 200 soldiers and artisans, starts construction of Fort Caroline under French flag.

1565, August 28—Ribault arrives at Fort Caroline with relief expedition of 600 settlers and soldiers.

1565, September 8—The Spanish establish the settlement of St. Augustine.

1565, September–October—The Spanish massacre about 300 French troops and civilians in two separate events at Matanzas, near the southern tip of Anastasia Island, because the Protestant French troops refused conversion to Catholicism.

1586—Sir Francis Drake leads expedition attacking St. Augustine.

1656—Franciscan friars establish mission at San Luis in Apalachee territory.

Spanish claims to Florida were supported by the explorations of Juan Ponce de León in 1513. The exact location of his first landing in Florida is still in dispute. (Engraving from *Die illustrierte neue welt*, New York, H. Bill, 1858. Courtesy of the Library of Congress.)

1671—The Spanish have a wooden watchtower built at site of Fort Matanzas.

1672—Castillo de San Marcos, the first fort built of coquina, is begun in St. Augustine.

1679—The Spanish build first log fort at location of Fort San Marcos de Apalache.

1690s—Palisade built around fort at Mission San Luis.

1702–13—Queen Anne's War is fought; British troops fight both Spanish and French in North America.

1702—British forces burn St. Augustine; residents take shelter in Castillo de San Marcos.

1704—Apalachee residents at Mission San Luis burn the fort and mission and flee ahead of British invasion.

1718—Spanish Capt. Jose Primo de Ribera leads construction of second wooden fort at site of San Marcos de Apalache.

1731, April 9—British sea captain Robert Jenkins, in command of ship *Rebecca*, is stopped by Spanish authorities off Havana; in the ensuing argument his ear is severed; eight years later, the incident precipitates a war.

Hernando de Soto first landed at Tampa Bay in 1539, as depicted in this 1853 engraving. (James Smillie, after a drawing by Capt. S. Eastman. Courtesy of the Library of Congress.)

Hernando de Soto led an expedition along the west coast of Florida in 1540, stopping at several locations including the Wakulla River spot where Pánfilo de Narváez had stopped in 1528 and where the Spanish later erected Fort San Marcos de Apalache. (Engraving by J. Maca, n.d. Courtesy of the Library of Congress.)

This engraving of Pensacola harbor was made in the 1770s, when Florida was under British control. (Published by George Gauld, London. Courtesy of the Library of Congress.)

1733—The British colony of Georgia is established by George Oglethorpe.

1738—Estimated free African population in St. Augustine reaches 100; 2 miles north of the city, the Spanish establish a free black community named Gracia Real de Santa Theresa de Mose.

1739—Stone construction begins at San Marcos de Apalache.

1739–48—War of Jenkins' Ear is fought.

1740–42—The Spanish build Fort Matanzas.

1740, June 26—After abandoning Fort Mose to the British, black troops recapture the fort in a surprise attack.

1743, March—Oglethorpe fails in attack on Castillo de San Marcos.

1748—Treaty of Aix-la-Chappelle ends the War of Jenkins' Ear and sets the boundary between Florida and Georgia at the St. Johns River.

1756–63—Seven Years' War; Spain cedes Florida to Britain in 1763 in order to regain control of Havana, Cuba, which the British had captured during that war.

1764—The Spanish evacuate free African Americans from Fort Mose to Cuba; British take possession of Florida and Spanish forts in the colony; the British rename Castillo de San Marcos as Fort St. Marks.

1764–83—Under British control, Florida is divided into East Florida, with its capital at St. Augustine, and West Florida, with its capital at Pensacola.

1768—Minorcans arrive at New Smyrna Colony located south of St. Augustine.

1775–81—American Revolution is fought.

1779—Spanish enter the war on the side of the American Patriots against the British.

1781, February 13—Bernardo de Gálvez leads a Spanish force to take Pensacola from British.

1781, May 5—Spanish artillery obliterates British-held Fort George in Pensacola.

1783–1821—The Spanish regain control of Florida under Treaty of Paris, which ends the American Revolution.

1787—The Spanish take over Fort San Marcos de Apalache after British evacuation.

1793–97—The Spanish build Fort Barrancas in Pensacola (now the water battery).

1800—British adventurer William Augustus Bowles establishes independent "republic of the Muskogee Nation" and attempts to seize Fort San Marcos de Apalache from Spanish garrison; Bowles is captured and sent to prison in Havana, Cuba, where he dies in 1805.

1812–15—War of 1812 is fought.

1814, August—The British begin training "Corps of Colonial Militia" on Apalachicola River in West Florida, made up of Seminole and African American forces.

1815—The British evacuate West Florida, leaving Corps of Colonial Militia in possession of supplies at the "Negro Fort."

1816, July 17—U.S. forces attempt attack on the Negro Fort on the Apalachicola River; four U.S. soldiers are killed.

1816, July 27—Andrew Jackson orders expedition under Gen. E. P. Gaines that destroys the Negro Fort; orders Fort Gadsden built at the site.

1817–18—Pirate Luis Aury sets up independent government at Fernandina on Amelia Island.

1818—Andrew Jackson leads attack on Fort San Marcos de Apalache and occupies the fort; U.S. forces rename it Fort St. Marks.

1818, April 29—Jackson has British subjects Robert Ambrister and Alexander Arbuthnot executed at Fort San Marcos de Apalache (Fort St. Marks).

1821—Spain cedes Florida to the United States in the Adams-Onis Treaty.

1824—U.S. troops turn over Fort San Marcos de Apalache (Fort St. Marks) to the Territory of Florida.

1824, December—U.S. Navy Commodore David Porter surveys Dry Tortugas as possible fort site; he recommends against it.

1825—U.S. government renames Castillo de San Marcos as Fort Marion.

1826—Lighthouse constructed on Garden Key, later the site of Fort Jefferson.

1829—U.S. Army engineers begin construction of Forts McRee, Pickens, Barrancas, and the Advanced Redoubt to protect Pensacola.

1829—U.S. Navy Commodore John Rodgers inspects Dry Tortugas and recommends construction of fort, later built as Fort Jefferson.

1834—Fort Pickens is completed.

1835, December 28—Osceola kills Indian agent Wiley Thompson at Fort King.

1835, December 28—Dade Battle and Osceola's killing of Indian agent Wiley Thompson initiate the Second Seminole War.

1835–42—Second Seminole War is fought.

1836, April—U.S. troops and Georgia Volunteers under command of Maj. Mark Anthony Cooper are besieged at an encampment at Lake Holathlikaha, just south of present-day Inverness; the spot was later named Fort Cooper in his honor.

1836, November 21—Battle of Wahoo Swamp is fought.

1837, January 20 and February 3—Seminole forces attack militia encamped at Fort Foster and attempt to burn the bridge over the Hillsborough River.

1837, October 1—Osceola is captured by U.S. troops.

1837, December 25—U.S. and Alabama volunteers under Gen. Abraham Eustis set up camp at what is later designated Fort Christmas.

1838—Steamer *Irvington* explodes in Apalachicola River; wreckage believed to be from this steamer is now on site of Fort Gadsden.

1838, January 30—Osceola dies in prison at Fort Moultrie, South Carolina.

1842—U.S. government purchases land for construction of Fort Clinch.

1845—U.S. government purchases 62.89 acres in Key West for construction of Fort Zachary Taylor.

1845, March 3—Florida is admitted to the Union as a state.

1846—Construction begins at Fort Jefferson.

1847—Construction begins at Fort Clinch.

1847, July 10—Seven slaves attempt escape from Fort Jefferson; they are later caught at present-day Marathon Key.

1848—Fort Pickens is abandoned.

1849, October—Line of forts across Florida, including Fort Chokonikla (Paynes Creek), are built to restrict remaining Seminoles south of the line.

1855, December 20—Third Seminole War (Billy Bowlegs' War) begins.

1857—Marine Hospital is built on site of Fort San Marcos de Apalache.

1858, May—Bowlegs' band surrenders, ending Third Seminole War.

1860, December 20—South Carolina formally declares secession from the United States and announces that it is an independent republic.

1861–65—American Civil War/War Between the States is fought.

1861—Florida militia occupy Fort Clinch.

1861—Confederates rename Fort San Marcos de Apalache (St. Marks) as Fort Ward.

1861, January 7—Florida convention officially announces secession from the United States; Castillo de San Marcos (Fort Marion) is peacefully turned over to state militia by U.S. Army.

1861, January 8—Gunshots fired at Fort Barrancas in Florida are "pre-first" shots of Civil War; Union troops reoccupy Fort Pickens.

1861, February 4—South Carolina, Georgia, Alabama, Mississippi, Florida, and Louisiana form the Confederate States of America after each separately announced secession from the United States. Texas joins later; Virginia, North Carolina, Arkansas, and Tennessee secede and join the Confederacy after the firing on Fort Sumter.

1861, March—U.S. troops resupply Fort Pickens.

1861, April 12—Firing on Fort Sumter marks the official start of Civil War.

1861, August 31—Union forces burn dry dock at Pensacola harbor.

1861, October 9—Gen. Braxton Bragg leads unsuccessful Confederate assault on Fort Pickens known as the Battle of Santa Rosa Island.

1861, November 21—Gun battles between U.S. Navy and Confederate States Army lead to near-destruction of Fort McRee.

1862, March 2—Confederate troops evacuate Fort Clinch without a battle.

1862, March 2—U.S. gunboat *Ottawa* fires on Confederate steam train near Fort Clinch.

1862, March 11—Troops from Union ship *Wabash* peacefully retake Castillo de San Marcos after Confederates evacuate March 10.

1862, April 10—Union guns demolish walls at Fort Pulaski, Georgia, demonstrating masonry walls are no protection against exploding shells.

1863—East and West Martello Towers are built in Key West.

1865, March 5—Battle of Natural Bridge, Florida, prevents Union forces from taking Tallahassee, the only Confederate state capital east of the Mississippi not to be taken by the Union.

1865, April 9 Lee surrenders his forces at Appomattox Court House, marking the end of major hostilities of the Civil War.

1865, July—Four of the Lincoln assassination conspirators are confined to prison at Fort Jefferson; three survivors pardoned in 1869.

1866—West Martello Tower in Key West abandoned.

1873—East Martello Tower in Key West abandoned.

1875–76—Hurricanes destroy part of Fort Zachary Taylor.

1875–78—Castillo de San Marcos (Fort Marion) used as prison for Native American warriors captured in U.S. West.

1877—Metal lighthouse constructed at Fort Jefferson.

1882—Military reservations are established on Mullet and Egmont Keys near Tampa; Mullet Key later becomes site of Fort De Soto.

1885–86—Endicott Plan for refurbishing seacoast forts is developed.

1886–87—Chiricahua Apache Indian leader Geronimo is imprisoned in Fort Pickens.

1887—Henry Flagler builds Hotel Ponce de Leon (now Flagler College) in St. Augustine.

1888–1900—Fort Jefferson is used as a quarantine station.

1889—A quarantine station is opened on Mullet Key near Tampa Bay.

1890—Double quarters are built at Key West Naval Station for base commander and the paymaster; later becomes Truman Little White House.

1898—Fort De Soto is built to protect embarkation of troops from Tampa for Cuba.

Before the firing on Fort Sumter, Union troops successfully came to resupply Fort Pickens as shown in these 1861 scenes from *Frank Leslie's Illustrated Newspaper*. (Courtesy of the Library of Congress.)

1898—Batteries Cullum, Sevier, and Van Swearingen are added at Fort Pickens.

1898, April 25—Spanish-American War begins.

1898, August 12—Spanish-American War ends.

1898—Battery A of Sixth Artillery occupies Fort Clinch; the troops evacuate after end of Spanish-American War in September.

1899, June 20—Fire and explosion destroy part of wall at Fort Pickens; ruins of that corner of the fort remain today.

1899—Battery Pensacola and Battery Worth are added at Fort Pickens (abandoned 1934).

1900—Fort De Soto is officially opened as a detachment of Fort Dade on Egmont Key.

1904—Battery Payne is added at Fort Pickens.

1905—Battery Trueman is added at Fort Pickens.

1906—Construction of gun emplacements at Fort De Soto completed.

1906—Battery Cooper is added at Fort Pickens.

1910—Fort De Soto is abandoned.

1911—Base commander's dwelling at Key West Naval Station converted to single-family home.

1912, December—President William Howard Taft stays at Key West Naval Station; first use of commandant's residence as presidential winter home.

1914–18—First World War is fought, beginning August 4, 1914.

1916—First funding for restoration of Fort Matanzas is approved.

1917, April 6—United States enters into World War I.

1917–18—Fort De Soto is reactivated; four heavy mortars are shipped to San Diego.

1918, November 11—Armistice is declared ending World War I.

1920s—The "Cracker era" in Florida is ill-defined, but most cultural historians use the term to refer to the cattle culture that began in the 1760s under British rule and extended to the 1920s.

1923—Battery Langdon added at Fort Pickens.

1923, May 25—Fort De Soto and Fort Dade (Egmont Key) are retired from active service.

1924—Fort Marion (Castillo de San Marcos) is designated a National Monument.

1924—Fort Matanzas is designated a National Monument.

1926—U.S. government sells Fort Clinch to private owners.

1933—Fort Marion is transferred from the War Department to the National Park Service.

1933—Fort Matanzas is transferred from the War Department to the National Park Service.

1934—Battery 234 added at Fort Pickens.

1935—State of Florida purchases Fort Clinch; CCC does work on park trails and restoration in Fort Clinch State Park.

1935, January 4—After a visit by yacht, President Franklin D. Roosevelt declares Fort Jefferson a National Monument.

1936—Fort Foster State Park is opened; gatehouse built by CCC later becomes the interpretive center.

1937—Battery GPF is added at Fort Pickens.

1938—War Department sells Fort De Soto to Pinellas County.

1939, September 1—Germany invades Poland, beginning World War II.

1940—U.S. War Department takes over Camp Blanding from State National Guard; it is converted to a major advanced infantry training center for the duration of World War II.

1941, June—War Department buys back Fort De Soto from Pinellas County; it is attached to MacDill Air Force Base and used as a bombing range until 1945.

1941, December 7—Japanese bomb Pearl Harbor, bringing United States into World War II.

1942—Fort Marion's name is changed back to Castillo de San Marcos.

1945, May 8—Germany surrenders.

1945, September 15—Japan surrenders, ending World War II.

1946, November—President Harry S. Truman visits what becomes the Truman Little White House (or his Winter White House) in Key West; he stays a total of 175 days over the next seven years.

1947—Fort Pickens is closed as active fort.

1947—War Department releases East and West Martello Towers in Key West to Monroe County; in the same action, the War Department releases Fort Zachary Taylor to the U.S. Navy.

1948—Pinellas County repurchases Fort De Soto from the War Department.

1949—Order for Defense Unification is signed at Truman Little White House, Key West.

1950, September 21—Fort Caroline is declared a National Memorial.

1951—Key West Art and Historical Society takes over East Martello Tower.

1953, January 16—Fort Caroline is officially opened for visitors.

1955—Key West Garden Club takes over West Martello Tower.

1962, November 26—President John F. Kennedy visits Truman Little White House in Key West.

1962, December 21—Pinellas County opens Fort De Soto for visitors; dedication follows on May 11, 1963.

1963, June 8—National Museum of Naval Aviation opens at the Pensacola Naval Base.

1966—Fort San Marcos de Apalache declared a National Historic Landmark.

1966—Castillo de San Marcos is listed on the National Register of Historic Places.

1968—U.S. Navy turns over Fort Zachary Taylor for restoration as part of Florida State Park system.

1971—Fort Barrancas becomes part of Gulf Islands National Seashore.

1972—Fort Pickens becomes part of the Gulf Islands National Seashore.

1973—Site of Fort Foster is deeded to State of Florida.

1976—Fort Pickens is opened to the public by the National Park Service.

1977, December 17—Replica of Fort Christmas is dedicated and opened by Orange County Parks and Recreation Commission.

1978—Fort Gadsden is taken over and administered by the U.S. Forest Service.

1978—Fort Chokonikla is placed on Register of Historic Places.

1978—Mortar batteries at Fort De Soto are placed on Register of Historic Places.

1980—Fort Barrancas is opened to public by National Park Service.

1981—Fort Chokonikla/Paynes Creek is opened to the public.

1983–86—Archaeological team uncovers Fort Mose artifacts.

1985—Air Force Armament Museum at Eglin Air Force Base is opened to the public.

1986, September 10—Developer Pritam Singh purchases 43 acres of Key West Naval Station; he later builds luxury housing in the Truman Annex and donates the Truman Little White House and its grounds to the State of Florida on January 1, 1987.

1992—President George H. W. Bush upgrades Fort Jefferson from National Monument to National Park.

1994—Fort Mose is listed on National Register of Historic Places.

2005—Hurricane Katrina destroys access road to Fort Pickens; the road is reopened for access by 2008.

Glossary

Adams-Onis Treaty—Negotiated in 1819 and ratified in 1821. Under this treaty, Spain ceded Florida to the United States, and the United States relinquished claims to Texas. The treaty also set the western boundary of the United States. Also known as the Transcontinental Treaty.

alternative use—In the case of some historic facilities, the whole facility or part of it has been converted to a modern alternative use. In Key West, Florida, the East Martello Tower has been converted to a museum and art gallery, while the West Martello Tower has been converted to a horticultural display of tropical and subtropical plants. These are the only forts described in this guidebook that have alternative-use status; others are either restored, preserved, or are replicas.

Apalachee—The Native American people who lived in northwest Florida when the Spanish arrived in the sixteenth century. Many converted to Christianity and lived in settled mission communities operated by Dominican friars and protected with small garrisons of Spanish troops. Their story is told at Mission San Luis.

artifact—An identified and authentic object from the past that can help to document the era. Artifacts such as weapons, tools, cooking utensils, furniture, costumes, and ornamentation are usually not presented for handling at historic sites, but are for display only. However, sometimes specially labeled displays are interactive, presenting reproductions or original artifacts for handling and educational use.

barbette—A raised-mound gun position within a fort allowing guns to be fired over a wall, rather than through embrasures. A gun so mounted was mounted *en barbette.*

bastion—In masonry forts, a pointed corner that made defense easier and attack more difficult. It allowed defenders to have a good view of the surrounding ground and to defend the walls that met at the bastion-protected corner by being able to see and fire weapons along the front of those walls.

battery—In gunnery, an arrangement of several artillery pieces in a group. In some forts in the early twentieth century, artillery batteries were named after military heroes, such as Battery Adair and Battery Osceola at Fort Zachary Taylor, and Battery Laidley and Battery Bigelow at Fort De Soto.

berm—Any raised earthen mounded ridge; in a fort, it was used as an outer defensive perimeter. Defensive berms can be seen at Castillo de San Marcos and at Fort Clinch.

blockhouse—In wooden or log forts, a two-story structure in which the second story projects beyond the walls of the first story to allow better firing positions against attackers. Blockhouses can be seen at Fort Foster and Fort Christmas.

canister shot—Also known as "case shot," canister shot consisted of a thin metal container, packed with lead balls and sawdust, that would disperse on firing and serve as antipersonnel projectiles. When lead shot was in scarce supply, a canister could be filled with scrap metal, nails, and even stones.

casemate—A room in a masonry outer wall of a fort devoted to a gun emplacement, usually constructed with arched roofs to bear the weight of the thick protective masonry or brick walls. At the end of the Civil War, some casemate rooms in coastal forts were converted to prison cells for important prisoners, as at Fort Jefferson.

cheveaux de frise—A defensive structure consisting of a movable obstacle made up of wooden or metal spikes attached to a wooden frame; used to fend off cavalry.

Civilian Conservation Corps (CCC)—A federal agency created as part of the New Deal under President Franklin Roosevelt; it operated from 1933 to 1942. The goal of the CCC was to hire unemployed young men, mostly from the cities, and enlist them in construction projects in state and national parks around the country. The "CCC boys" lived under a semi-military regimen, camping in barracks and tent encampments, and working in the open air to build trails, park buildings and facilities. The characteristic CCC style of architecture employed rough-hewn logs and rustic details. CCC crews helped repair or build facilities at several Florida forts.

Cheveaux de-frize, large joints or beams, ſtuck full of wooden pins, armed with iron, to ſtop breaches, or to ſecure a paſſage of a camp againſt the enemy's cavalry.

A *cheveaux de frise*, easily constructed of pointed or iron-tipped sticks, was an excellent defensive line against infantry. (*A new military, historical, and explanatory dictionary*, by Thomas Simes, Philadelphia, 1776. Courtesy of the Library of Congress.)

columbiad—The term for a seacoast defensive gun or howitzer of an extremely large size that fired explosive shells eight or more inches in diameter. The term came into use in 1844 to describe these weapons, which were made over the period 1839–57.

Confederacy—Eleven states voted to secede from the United States in 1860–61. In February 1861, they formed the Confederate States of America, or the Confederacy. The resultant war to restore these states to the Union was known in the United States as the Civil War (1861–65), and within the Confederacy as the War Between the States. Battles at Fort Pickens, at Natural Bridge, and at the Olustee Battlefield were major conflicts in the Civil War, while the forts on the seacoast were actively used by the Union forces in the blockade of Florida.

coquina—A local building material consisting of compressed shells, found and quarried on Anastasia Island and other coastal islands and used in the building of Castillo de San Marcos, Fort Matanzas, and other structures. The overgrown remnants of a coquina quarry can be found in Anastasia Island State Park. Coquina is a sedimentary rock akin to limestone or sandstone, but made of compacted coquina shell. It is mined from natural deposits, cut into slabs or blocks, and left to cure or harden for up to a year so that the rock loses moisture and sets.

counterscarp wall—In forts with an outer wall and an inner wall enclosing a ditch or moat, the outer wall, known as the counterscarp, could support a mounded earthworks, known as a glacis. A tunnel under the ditch allowed troops to have access to a counterscarp gallery within the wall for firing at enemy troops who might have gained access to the ditch. This arrangement can be viewed at Fort Barrancas.

Cracker house—From the 1870s through the mid-twentieth century, early settlers' homes in Florida were often built very economically, and a characteristic form emerged: one story, wood construction, raised off the ground with a crawlspace below, with an overhanging roof projecting over a front porch. The Cracker house typically had two to four small rooms. The term "Cracker" applied to settlers of this era, is thought to derive from the long cattle whips that cowboys cracked over cattle as they drove them overland. In several sites around Florida, small "Cracker house villages" have been erected as historic attractions, usually by transporting already-built houses and other buildings to the site, restoring them, and furnishing them with period artifacts.

crenellation—The alternating raised and lower sections found in some fort and castle walls. The raised sections are **merlins**, and the lower sections are **crenels** or **embrasures**, through which defenders could fire on approaching enemy troops. Castillo de San Marcos at St. Augustine has a crenellated wall. The parapet with crenellation is sometimes called a *battlement*.

cunnette—A drainage ditch. A brick-lined cunnette is found in the dry moat at the Advanced Redoubt at Fort Barrancas.

curtain wall—The outside sloped or vertical wall of a fort.

Dahlgren guns—Named after the naval officer John A. Dahlgren, who first designed them in 1854, these large cannons have a characteristic soda-bottle shape. The large breech or back end was designed to be able to withstand the pressures of the exploding charge and could therefore accommodate a larger powder charge than could a straight tubular design. No Dahlgren gun ever blew up while in service.

demibastion—At some forts, a slightly angled bastion would provide gun ports that could provide withering fire on enemy troops approaching the main entrance or sally port. Such demibastions can be seen at the Advanced Redoubt at Fort Barrancas.

diorama—In museum displays, dioramas are illustrative reconstructions, either on full-scale or on a miniaturized scale, of an event or a process, such as the construction of a building or the daily lifestyle of the inhabitants of a community or of wildlife. Dioramas are so called because there are two levels of presentation, with the figurines (or stuffed animals) placed against a painted background to give the impression of depth.

dungeon—An underground inner room of a fort or castle, sometimes windowless, that could easily be converted for the confinement of prisoners.

embrasure—The firing indentation in a parapet or wall, also known as a **crenel** when on the upper parapet wall. Embrasures for cannons would often be wider on the outside than on the inside, to allow a wide arc for the cannon barrel to be swiveled, thus to gain a wider field of fire.

Endicott Plan—The Endicott Board (convened and chaired by Secretary of War William Endicott) recommended dispersed guns, concealed emplacements, and exploding ordnance. In 1885 the War Department convened the Joint Army-Navy Board on Fortifications and Other Defenses, known as the Endicott Board. The report of this board, known as the Endicott Plan, was some 391 pages long. It shaped the development of American coastal ordnance for the next thirty years. The plan called for more than $90 million in improvements to coastal defense, but by 1895, only some $10 million had been spent.

escarpment—The inner wall of a moat or ditch that had to be climbed during attack.

fascine—A bound bundle of sticks used to strengthen earthworks or the sides of trenches.

French and Indian War—In this war, fought between 1754 and 1763, the French lost possession of Canada, and the Spanish lost possession of Florida, both to the British. Under the Peace of Fontainebleau, Florida was ceded to England in trade for Havana, Cuba, that had fallen under British control. Also known as the Seven Years' War in Europe, where it began in 1756, two years later than it did in North America.

gabion—A basket made of woven sticks, to contain earth or rocks to reinforce a defensive position.

gallery—In a fort or fortress, a gallery is a tunnel-like hallway connecting an outer defensive position such as bastion or the curtain wall, with the interior of the fort. Such galleries can be seen at several Florida forts, including Barrancas and Clinch.

glacis—An artificial slope of earth placed around the outer walls or ditches of a fort, so that approaching enemy foot soldiers could be more readily targeted from within the fort. A good example of a glacis slope can be seen at Fort Clinch. A glacis slope concealing the fort itself is found at Fort Barrancas.

howitzer—A gun that would fire shells with a medium or low velocity, but at a high-angled trajectory.

Huguenots—French Protestants. Huguenots and Catholics fought a series of civil wars, with massacres on both sides, through the years 1562–98. The original settlers at Fort Caroline were Huguenots who sought to escape persecution in France.

interpreter or **costumed interpreter**—At historic sites, an interpreter is a guide who wears a costume of the era of the site, and is well informed about the events and history of the site. In some cases, an interpreter will play the role of a specific historic person or type of person; sometimes they are engaged in a handicraft or other work of the period they are representing to visitors.

loophole—A vertical, narrow slot in a defensive tower or wall, cut through the wall at an angle wider on the inside and more narrow outside, so that defenders would be able to aim their hand-held weapons over a wide arc, while offering only a very small target for attacking forces. Also called **arrow-slits, arrow loops**, or **rifle** or **musket loopholes**, depending on the weaponry used.

magazine—An inner room or underground chamber devoted to the storage of gunpowder.

mannequin—A dummy used to display costumes or to represent a historic personage in historic displays; mannequins are used at the museums at Camp Blanding and Fort De Soto.

Martello tower—A seacoast battery tower, usually armed with one to four cannon on the top of the tower that would cover a field of fire in any 360-degree position. Two such Martello towers are located in Key West, Florida.

Mikasuki—A dialect of the Muscogean languages, spoken by indigenous people of Alabama and Georgia; among the Seminoles, it was spoken along with Creek, another Muscogean language; Hitchiti was another closely related Muscogean language, now extinct.

A mortar being swabbed out by Connecticut troops in the Civil War. (Drawing by Alfred R. Waud, 1864. Courtesy of the Library of Congress.)

moat—A defensive ditch surrounding a castle or fort. Depending on location, a moat could be kept dry and flooded during an attack, or kept permanently filled with water to deter attack. Also known as a **foss.**

mortar—When referring to a gun, a mortar is a muzzle-loading gun that fires a shell in a high arc, for a short range, and with low velocity. Nineteenth-century siege mortars were often immobile, low, and squat, and would have an outside barrel diameter many times the diameter of the inside bore, used to defend a fort during siege by bombarding any attacking forces with shells dropping nearly vertically on them.

musket—A smooth-bore, long-barreled, hand-held gun that would be loaded at the muzzle. With practice, a soldier could load and fire a musket shot every twenty to thirty seconds. The weapons were not at all accurate, so they were most effective when several (or many) soldiers fired simultaneously at a target, accounting for the practice of lining troops up to fire a volley at opposing troops. This tactic was characteristic of warfare in the eighteenth and early nineteenth centuries.

Paixhan guns—These naval guns were designed by the French gun designer Henri-Joseph Paixhan in 1823, and were the first naval guns to fire explosive (rather than solid) shot. Many guns over the nineteenth century that fired explosive shells were known as Paixhan guns. Such weapons rendered the Third System of Fortifications obsolete, even as some of the forts of that system were under construction.

palisade—A wooden barrier wall around a fort using sharpened vertical logs; a palisade is found at the fort at Mission San Luis.

parade or **parade ground**—The level space within a fort or fortification.

parapet—A wall on the upper edge of a fortress, behind which guns would be placed, sometimes cut through with crenellation.

pilaster buttress—A buttress is a sloping or arched support for a wall. A pilaster buttress is directly joined to the wall with no arched space beneath it, and it is flat and wide at the base narrowing and sloping toward the top. Such buttresses are found at Castillo de San Marcos.

Queen Anne's War *(1702–13)*—Known in Europe as the War of Spanish Succession, Great Britain fought against both France and Spain; in North America, the war resulted in the French losing Acadia, Newfoundland, and Hudson Bay (in what is now Canada), and the island of St. Kitts in the Caribbean. The British invasion of Florida resulted in the destruction of Spanish missions among the Apalachee and Timucua Native Americans, and the abandonment of Mission San Luis.

rampart—An outer defensive perimeter of a fort made of a raised earthen berm.

redoubt—A protected position. The Advanced Redoubt at Fort Barrancas is quite unique in that it was a fort in itself, designed to protect the major fort from land attack.

replica—A replica building is one constructed along the lines of an older structure, using similar (or identical) designs and plans. A replica is distinct from a preserved, reconstructed, or original building, in that it has been constructed in modern times to represent a structure from a previous era for display purposes. Replica structures are found at Fort Caroline, Fort Cooper, Fort Christmas, Fort Foster, and Mission San Luis.

reenactor—At a historic site such as a battlefield or fort, a reenactor is a costumed volunteer who wears the uniform or other costume of the period. Large groups of reenactors often will present a whole battle in a **reenactment**, complete with the firing of handheld weapons (with blank charges) such as muskets and rifles, and sometimes including such features as cavalry charges, Native American skirmishes, and the firing of artillery. Sometimes reenactors step out of their character and role to present an interpretive lecture or discussion about a battle or period, and in that activity, they are similar to costumed interpreters. Reenactors often stay at a historic site in an encampment, complete with tents, fire pits, cooking implements, and other equipment characteristic of the period they represent. When not engaged in a mock battle, most reenactors will gladly answer detailed questions about uniforms, equipment, and the historical event that they are reenacting.

reverse arch—When heavy brick or masonry walls were constructed on a sand base, a reverse arch, or curved masonry or brick support, would sometimes be built underneath doorways and other arched openings. An excavated reverse arch can be viewed at Fort Pickens.

Rodman guns—A series of heavy guns designed by Union artilleryman Thomas Jackson Rodman in the Civil War era. They could fire both solid shot and explosive shell. These guns were intended to be mounted in seacoast fortifications, and they had bores of 8-inch, 10-inch, 13-inch, 15-inch, and 20-inch diameters. The guns all had a curving soda-bottle shape, with large projections with ratchets or sockets for the elevating mechanism. Rodman guns were unique in the era because they were hollow cast, a technology that Rodman had personally developed, leading to guns that were much stronger than earlier ones. No Rodman gun ever exploded in service. They were cast at the Naval gun foundry at the Washington Navy Yard. Six 15-inch Rodman guns can be seen at Fort Jefferson, while numerous 10-inch Rodmans can be seen at Fort Clinch, Fort Taylor, and Fort Pickens.

sally port (or **sallieport**)—The main (usually the only) entrance to a castle or fort.

scarp—Another term for the outer, main curtain wall of a fort or fortress, usually built nearly vertically, to prevent scaling by attacking enemy troops.

scarp cordon—An overhanging ridge, built below the embrasures on a fort, to prevent besieging troops from scaling the wall. A scarp cordon was used at Fort Matanzas for just such a purpose.

scarp gallery—A gallery or long hallway built within the inner major wall of a fort, from which troops could fire on attacking enemy soldiers who might have penetrated that far into the fort's defenses. A scarp gallery can be seen at Fort Barrancas.

Seminole—The name for the Native American peoples who lived in Florida from the late 1700s onward. They were mostly related to the Creek peoples of Georgia and Alabama. The term "seminole" is thought to derive from the Spanish word *cimarron* which meant "wild" or "runaway." The same Spanish word was also the root for the term "maroons," referring to communities of runaway slaves who established settlements in remote or inaccessible lands of the Caribbean and the United States. Among the Seminoles, runaway African American slaves from Georgia and South Carolina settled. These people were known as Afro-Seminoles or Seminole African American allies. A number of European-descended settlers also intermarried with the Seminoles.

Seminole Wars—Three wars between U.S. Army forces and the Seminole Native Americans: First Seminole War 1817–18; Second Seminole War 1835–42; Third Seminole War 1855–58 (also known as Billy Bowlegs' War). For further detail, see the entries in this guidebook for Fort Cooper and for Dade Battlefield.

sentry tower—A small, round tower built at the corners or bastions of a fort, from which defenders could fire on attackers with firearms or other weapons. Such towers are prominent at Castillo de San Marcos.

Spanish-American War—War fought between April and August 1898 in which the United States acquired Puerto Rico and the Philippines from Spain, and liberated Cuba from Spanish rule.

spiked guns—To render a captured gun useless, a metal spike would be driven into the powder ignition hole, requiring a long delay for the spike to be drilled out.

stockade—A wall constructed of logs standing vertically, also known as a **palisade.** Notable examples in Florida can be seen at Fort Foster and Fort Christmas.

tabby—A form of colonial concrete or cement; it is not natural, but is made by mixing lime, sand, and water to make cement, or these

This 1898 photo from a stereopticon slide shows troops departing from the docks at Tampa for the Cuban front in the Spanish-American War. (Strohmeyer & Wyman publishers, New York, N.Y., ca. 1898. Courtesy of the Library of Congress.)

ingredients plus an aggregate like whole oyster shell, to make concrete, and poured into molds or forms to harden.

terreplein—The roof over the inner wall and outer wall of a fort, where guns could be mounted and defenders could fire over the parapet at attackers. More generally, the term refers to any floor that is in a plane parallel to the level of the ground. The terreplein at Castillo de San Marcos is open for visitors.

Third System of Fortifications (1821–60)—In 1794 and 1807, before Florida became part of the United States, the U.S. Congress appropriated money for fortifications to guard key harbors. The forts that were built with these funds were the First and Second Systems of American seacoast fortification. Many of these forts

This lithograph shows Fort Barnwell with a stockade surrounding the fort. (T. F. Gray and James, Charleston, S.C., 1837. Courtesy of the Library of Congress.)

were not completed and soon deteriorated since they were usually built with earth with some masonry backing. In 1816, following the War of 1812, Congress appropriated more than $800,000 for new seacoast fortifications, and that amount funded the beginning of the Third System. Several of the forts in Florida, most notably Fort Jefferson, Fort Clinch, Fort Barrancas, Fort Pickens, and Fort Zachary Taylor were part of this Third System. The most familiar feature of the dozens of forts of the Third System were the large masonry structures built to contain many guns in their vertical exterior walls, usually overlooking and protecting a harbor or other waterway from attacking ships.

Timucua—The Native American people who lived in Florida in the 1500s. They eventually died out from disease and attacks by other Native American tribes. The population declined from possibly tens of thousands to an estimated 550 in 1698, and entirely vanished after that. The visitor center at Fort Caroline provides information on early Timucua life.

Totten shutters—Swinging iron shutters designed by General Joseph Gilbert Totten, chief of the U.S. Army Engineer Corps, just before the Civil War, after years of study. The shutters were mounted in front of fort gun ports or embrasures to protect the gunners from incoming small-arms fire. The shutters would swing out from the blast of air and gas when the cannon at the port was fired and swing back to protect the gunners from enemy musket

The Spanish observe a Timucua victory celebration. (1591 engraving by Theodor de Bry, after a watercolor by Jacques Le Moyne. Courtesy of the Library of Congress.)

Timucua villages were protected from attack by a circular wooden palisade, or stockade, with a narrow entrance passageway. (1591 engraving by Theodor de Bry, after a watercolor by Jacques Le Moyne. Courtesy of the Library of Congress.)

and small-arms fire. Found at Fort Jefferson. The fact that they rusted out and expanded as they rusted proved very destructive to the brick embrasure openings there.

water battery—An emplacement of several guns at water level for protecting harbors or docking areas. The guns could be fired on level, directly at any approaching enemy ships. A Spanish-built water battery can be seen at Fort Barrancas, and a water battery was also mounted at Castillo de San Marcos.

War of 1812—Fought 1812–15 between the United States and Great Britain.

War of Independence (American Revolutionary War)—Fought 1776–83. France was an ally of the American revolutionaries from 1778, and Spain was an ally from 1779. At the end of this war, Spain regained possession of Florida from Britain as part of the Paris Peace Treaty.

War of Jenkins' Ear—Fought 1739–48 between Spain and England. In this war, British forces under James Oglethorpe, the founder of Georgia, invaded Florida and unsuccessfully tried to capture the Castillo de San Marcos in St. Augustine from the Spanish. For more detail on this war, see the entry on Castillo de San Marcos.

Readings

Aptheker, Herbert. *American Negro Slave Revolts.* 1943. 5th ed. New York: International Publishers, 1983.

Bearrs, Edwin C. *Historical Structure Report, Fort Pickens Historical Data Section, 1821–1895.* Denver: U.S. Department of Interior, 1983.

Belko, William S. *America's Hundred Year War: U.S. Expansion to the Gulf Coast and the Fate of the Seminole, 1763–1858.* Gainesville: University Press of Florida, 2011.

Bennett, Charles E. *Laudonnière & Fort Caroline: History and Documents.* Huntsville: University of Alabama Press, 2001.

Coleman, James C., and Irene S. *Guardians on the Gulf: Pensacola Fortifications, 1698–1980.* Pensacola, Fla.: Pensacola Historical Society, 2000.

Deagan, Kathleen. *Fort Mose: Colonial America's Black Fortress.* Gainesville: University Press of Florida, 1995.

DeQuesada, A. M. *A History of Florida Forts: Florida's Lonely Outposts.* Charleston, S.C.: History Press, 2006.

Hann, John H., and Bonnie G. McEwan. *The Apalachee Indians and Mission San Luis.* Gainesville: University Press of Florida, 1998.

Heidler, David S., and Jeanne T. Heidler. *Old Hickory's War: Andrew Jackson and the Quest for Empire.* Mechanicsburg, Pa.: Stackpole Books, 1996.

Historic Print and Map Company. *The History of Castillo San Marcos.* St. Augustine, Fla.: Historic Print and Map Company, 2009.

Kaufman, J. E., and H. W. Kaufman. *Fortress America: The Forts That Defended America, 1600 to the Present.* Cambridge, Mass.: Da Capo Press, 2007.

Kleinberg, Eliot. *Historical Traveler's Guide to Florida.* Sarasota, Fla.: Pineapple Press, 2006.

Knetsch, Joe. *Florida in the Spanish American War.* With Nick Wynne. Charleston, S.C.: History Press, 2011.

———. *Florida's Seminole Wars, 1817–1858.* Charleston, S.C.: Arcadia, 2003.

Konstam, Angus. *American Civil War Fortifications (1): Coastal Brick and Stone Forts.* Oxford, U.K.: Osprey, 2003.

Landers, Jane. *Black Society in Spanish Florida.* Champaigne: University of Illinois Press, 1999.

Laumer, Frank. *Dade's Last Command.* Gainesville: University Press of Florida, 1995.

Lewis, Emanuel Raymond. *Seacoast Fortifications of the United States: An Introductory History.* Annapolis, Md.: U.S. Naval Institute Press, 1993.

Mahon, John K. *History of the Second Seminole War.* 1967. 2nd rev. ed., Gainesville: University Press of Florida, 1985.

McReynolds, Edwin C. *The Seminoles.* 1957. Norman: University of Oklahoma Press, 1972.

Milanich, Jerald T. *The Timucua.* Oxford, U.K.: Blackwell, 1996.

Missall, John, and Mary Lou Missall. *The Seminole Wars: America's Longest Indian Conflict.* Gainesville: University Press of Florida, 2004.

Mulroy, Kevin. *Freedom on the Frontier: The Seminole Maroons in Florida, the Indian Territory, Coahuila, and Texas.* Lubbock: Texas Tech University Press, 2003.

Nulty, William H. *Confederate Florida: The Road to Olustee.* Tuscaloosa: University of Alabama Press, 1994.

Porter, Kenneth W. *The Black Seminoles: A History of a Freedom-Seeking People.* Gainesville: University Press of Florida, 1996.

Reid, Thomas. *America's Fortress: A History of Fort Jefferson.* Gainesville: University Press of Florida, 2006.

Remini, Robert V. *Andrew Jackson and His Indian Wars.* New York: Viking Penguin, 2001.

Robson, Lucia St. Clair. *Light a Distant Fire.* London: Barrie and Jenkins, 1990.

Schellings, William J. "Key West and the Spanish American-War." *Tequesta* (Journal of the Southern Florida Historical Society), no. 20 (1960): 19–29.

Smith, W. Stanford. *Camp Blanding: Florida Star in Peace and War.* Fuquay-Varina, N.C.: Research Triangle Publishing, 1998.

Taylor, Paul. *Discovering the Civil War in Florida: A Reader and Guide.* Sarasota, Fla.: Pineapple Press, 2001.

Waterbury, Jean Parker, ed. *The Oldest City.* St. Augustine, Fla.: St. Augustine Historical Society, 1983.

Weisman, Brent R. *Unconquered People: Florida's Seminole and Miccosukee Indians.* Gainesville: University Press of Florida, 1999.

Index

Page numbers in boldface refer to main entries; page numbers in italics refer to illustrations.

Rodney Carlisle is professor emeritus at Rutgers University. He is author or editor of more than 40 volumes of historical works in social, political, and military history, including *Sovereignty at Sea: U.S. Merchant Ships and American Entry into World War I.*

Loretta Carlisle is a professional photographer, with illustrations appearing in multiple volumes of the series *One Day in History*, *Turning Points—Actual and Alternate Histories,* and *Handbook to Life in America*. In her spare time, she photographs nesting eagles and their young.

Rodney and Loretta Carlisle are collaborating on another project, a 500-year history of St. Augustine, Florida.

The University Press of Florida is the scholarly publishing agency for the State University System of Florida, comprising Florida A&M University, Florida Atlantic University, Florida Gulf Coast University, Florida International University, Florida State University, New College of Florida, University of Central Florida, University of Florida, University of North Florida, University of South Florida, and University of West Florida.